Discover the Power that Drives Your Personality: How Four Virtues Define Your World - An Introduction to the Life Themes: Love, Justice, Wisdom, Power

Discover the Power that Drives Your Personality: How Four Virtues Define Your World - An Introduction to the Life Themes: Love, Justice, Wisdom, Power

JOHN VORIS

JOHN VORIS
CARMEL, CA

Voris, John, *Discover The Power That Drives Your Personality: How Four Virtues Define Your World – Introduction to the Life Themes: Love, Justice, Wisdom, Power*

Copyright © 2019 John Voris

All rights reserved. This book or any portion thereof may not be reproduced or used in any manner whatsoever without the express written permission of the publisher, except for the use of brief quotations in a book review or scholarly journal.

First Printing: May 2019

ISBN: 978-1-7330525-0-4

John Voris

P.O. Box 5246

Carmel, CA 92321

www.JohnVoris.com

Contents

	Preface	1
	Acknowledgements	5
	Quote	7

Section I. Why Use the John Voris Method?

1.	The John Voris Method Explained	11
2.	The Four Life Themes	21

Section II. Learning the Life Themes

3.	Love: Advocates of Humanity	25
4.	Justice: Arbiters of Humanity	37
5.	Wisdom: Teachers of Humanity	49
6.	Power: Leaders of Humanity	59

Section III. Learning How the Life Themes Interact

7.	Interaction	71
8.	Love and Wisdom Interaction	79

9.	Love and Justice Interaction	83
10.	Love and Power Interaction	87
11.	Love and Love Interaction	91
12.	Wisdom and Justice Interaction	93
13.	Wisdom and Power Interaction	97
14.	Wisdom and Wisdom Interaction	101
15.	Justice and Power Interaction	103
16.	Justice and Justice Interaction	107
17.	Power and Power Interaction	109

Section IV. Putting the John Voris Method into Action In Your Life

18.	Why This is Not Another Personality Profiling Test	113
19.	Why the John Voris Method Works	115
20.	How to Use the John Voris Method in Your Life	117

Section V. About the Author

About Authentic Systems	123
Definitions	125
Love Life Theme	129
Wisdom Life Theme	131
Justice Life Theme	133
Power Life Theme	135

The Power of Four	137
Bibliography	149
Want to Learn More?	173

Preface

Tell the truth...Have you consulted with the sorting hat and asked which Harry Potter house you fit into? Do you know which city you should live in based on your personality? Or, in the "Friends" television show universe, have you determined if you are more like a Ross, Chandler, Joey, Monica, Rachel, or a Phoebe? According to Wired magazine, tens of millions of us take online quizzes like these on social media sites. These popular quizzes are supposed to give us more insight about ourselves. Buzzfeed's "What City Should You Live In?" quiz alone has attracted more than 20 million unique visitors.[1]

Online quizzes are well liked because we are fascinated with knowing who we really are. We love learning insights about ourselves. Most of us don't take their answers seriously, however, because they are just for fun and not based on scientific fact.

What about other personality profiling tests, such as the Myers Briggs Type Indicator? Shouldn't we take the results from these tests seriously?

According to the Washington Post, many people and companies do put a lot of stock in the personality profiling testing process and its results. "More than 10,000 companies, 2,500 colleges and universities and 200 government agencies in the United States use the Myers Briggs Type Indicator. It's estimated that 50 million people have taken the Myers-Briggs personality test since the Educational Testing Service first added the research to its portfolio in 1962."[2] The Myers Briggs Type Indicator is just one of thousands of personality profiling tests that individuals use.

If personality profile testing is so widely used, and is a part of the Educational Testing Service, it must be accurate, right?

Not so fast.

"Despite its widespread use and vast financial success, and although it was derived from the work of Carl Jung, one of the most famous psychologists of the 20th century, [personality profile testing] is highly questioned by the scientific community."[3]

Why? If we have so many quizzes, indicators, and personality profile tests, why are we still uncertain about who we are?

The answer is DOING versus BEING.

Let me ask you this. What describes you best – what you DO or what you ARE?

For example, when you are meeting someone new in America, one of the first questions they will ask you is, "What do you do?" It's expected that the answer will be what you do as a career or livelihood.

"I'm a real estate agent."

"I'm a doctor."

"I'm an accountant."

The answer is often treated as defining who you are as a person. However, the other person learns your occupation, but does your answer reveal anything about who you really are as a person?

No.

Reading and understanding this book will likely become a pivotal moment in your life.

Why?

What you are about to learn in this book will reveal who you really ARE. What you do can change but who you really ARE never changes.

The concepts in this book will completely change not only your understanding of who you are, but it will also teach you how to read and learn who other people are, too. You will learn the benefits and challenges of interacting with other people and who they really are.

By following the practical advice shared here, you will transform your relationships, your career, and more. It is a method that seems deceptively simple, and yet it is revolutionary and will turn everything you thought you knew about people and who they are on its head.

We introduce to you the John Voris method.

[1] https://www.wired.com/2014/03/buzzfeed-quizzes/

[2] https://www.washingtonpost.com/national/on-leadership/myers-briggs-does-it-pay-to-know-your-type/2012/12/14/eaed51ae-3fcc-11e2-bca3-aadc9b7e29c5_story.html?noredirect=on&utm_term=.ec6e944c3f0d

[3] https://www.washingtonpost.com/national/on-leadership/myers-briggs-does-it-pay-to-know-your-type/2012/12/14/eaed51ae-3fcc-11e2-bca3-aadc9b7e29c5_story.html?noredirect=on&utm_term=.ec6e944c3f0d

Acknowledgements

I would like to thank my daughters, Amanda and Jessica, for their developmental and artistic contributions; Linda Hardenstein, for sharing her expertise as a Career Consultant; Bill Lopachuk, for his inspiration; Rachelle Onishi for helping me structure my early workshops; Tom Burns, as my first formal reading; Dr. Russ Volkman, who helped me transition into consumer-friendly language; Bill Graham for launching my initial business structure; Melissa Wells, who assisted in preparing this book; Jean Ferguson, my administrative assistant; Jonathan Rogers, for his technical support and as a sounding board over the years. And of course I must mention with great fanfare, my editor and writing coach extraordinaire, Kim Eley.

"The Mind has only one need:
the perpetual need to express our Authentic Identity
through objects, relationships, and events."
–John W. Voris

SECTION I
WHY USE THE JOHN VORIS METHOD?

1. The John Voris Method Explained

WHO ARE YOU, REALLY?

It seems like such a simple question. When asked, "Who are you?", how do you describe yourself?

Most people in America respond with answers such as:

- I am a father
- I work as a realtor
- I am an American

These answers may describe what the person does, but they do not tell the whole story.

Why?

These characteristics do not reveal what we want, hope for, believe in, and care about. Yet it is these capacities that make us human. Western science focuses only on what is measurable, even when examining human nature. However, this approach is incomplete.

Science cannot penetrate our inner abstract minds.

Science tells us what we do. Personality tells us how we do it. The **John Voris Method** reveals why.

To live a fulfilling life we must examine who we are at a deeper level. But how do we remember what it means to be human? How do we discover who we really are?

WHY THE JOHN VORIS METHOD IS IMPORTANT

The **John Voris Method** is important because I reveal a person's truest essence and life purpose – what I call your **Life Theme**. Never before has there been a method that answers your deepest questions about who you are and your place in the world.

Through the **John Voris Method**, I uncover what gives your life:

- Happiness
- Meaning
- Purpose
- Belonging

Most people are not living out their intended Life Theme. Instead, they have designed an Identity Expression that includes partial authenticity.

What does that mean? Your Life Theme is always shadowed by your personality. Your personality is culturally driven based on how you or others believe you should act. But your Life Theme drives your authenticity.

Personality profiling tests tell you what you DO, but they do not tell you who you ARE. The personality test givers speculate who you "should" be from the answers you provide in a Personality Profile Test.

The John Voris Method reveals to you who you ARE.

THE METHOD'S BACKGROUND...AND WHY IT IS RADICALLY DIFFERENT

My interest was rooted from my own frustrations and failures while making a living selling products door to door. The same training I was given for sales was taught to every potential salesperson. Yet I noticed that some salespeople thrived, while others failed, all in the same environment. I wanted to know why.

I focused on discovering why people with similar backgrounds, opportunities, and intelligence levels succeeded or failed at certain occupations.

I finally answered my questions about failure and success but ended up going much deeper than just researching careers. Based on my lifetime of observation and research, by combining European psychology and philosophy, forensic science, anthropology, and archaeology, **I have discovered a type of Human Blueprint** that reveals what it is to be human and to capture what makes "you" distinctively "you."

The John Voris Method identifies the huge power structures that drive your personality – both known to you and hidden.

DISCOVERING YOUR DESIGN

I have trained myself to recognize your **Human Blueprint** which reveals your life purpose. The John Voris Method:

- Identifies the aspects of yourself that define who you **really** are using the discoveries of European scholars.
- Discovers your inherent design – what you are here to do and express
- Shows what you need in order to feel acknowledged and to experience genuine happiness as an individual.

I believe we are specifically designed with precision and intelligence. While my method is astonishingly accurate, it is not magic or done with psychic abilities. I use a series of questions that seem rather mundane. However, these questions are formulated to discover and assemble your unique personal symbols that describe your true nature.

Symbols and virtues you express hold the code to revealing your **Authentic Identity** hidden by your personality. **I am a detective solving the mystery of who you really are. The "clues" are the objects around you and your interactions with them.**

THE AUTHENTIC IDENTITY

The **Authentic Identity** is made up of energetic systems that interplay with one another generating stability and flexibility in your life revealing your:

- Living Design
- Life Purpose
- Interests
- Beliefs
- Values
- Virtues
- Motivations
- Judgements

There are four Universal Virtues:

- Love
- Justice
- Wisdom
- Power

All of us use each of these Universal Virtues in our lives. We learn in order to understand (Wisdom) the meaning of all that is in our environment; this learning occurs progressively through social exchanges to justify our decisions (Justice) and experiences with others as we act (Power) to produce and impact our environment. This is all dedicated to affirm (Love) our identity and promote well-being in the world.

My method identifies how these universal motivation systems design our lives.

THE LIFE THEME

While each of the Universal Virtues – Love, Justice, Wisdom, and Power – applies to everyone, only one of the Universal Virtues is the dominant force for each of us. This is known as our **Life Theme**.

This powerful Life Theme addresses for us:

- Validation
- What brings meaning to our lives
- How we belong socially
- What it means in our lives to make a difference
- Guidance for our lives
- The ability to experience joy and happiness

THE THREE UNIVERSAL FORMS OF SELF-EXPRESSION

Your Life Theme is the hidden ultimate foundation and anchor. These define the type and kind of beliefs and values driving your action. They form your intentions in life. Science has found that **how you express your Life Theme, or the way you express your Life Theme**, dominated by your fixed genetic predisposition usually seen as your outer personality.

There are three forms of self-expression:

1. **Authentically, through expressing our abstract ideas;**
2. **Synthetically, by how we physically express our authentic ideas through action and;**
3. **Temporarily, by briefly escaping from both through Rejuvenation.**

The John Voris Method enables you to identify these expressions of motivation which contribute to your individualistic design.

1. **Authentic Motivation**

Your Authentic Motivation is how you use your Life Theme to care for yourself and for others. It is a stable, timeless, and unchanging guide. It is the reason **WHY** you engage with the world the way you do. Simply, it is who you ARE throughout your lifetime. It is BEING who you are beneath life's changes.

2. **Synthetic Motivation**

Your Synthetic Motivation is seen as your external personality. This is **HOW** and **WHAT** you engage with in the world. It changes frequently. It is flexible so you can adapt to different situations when you engage with others. This is the more "public and social" part of you. Simply it is what you DO.

3. **Rejuvenating Motivation**

Since your mind is constantly crossing back and forth between **being** AUTHENTIC and SYNTHETIC **doing**, it gets exhausted. Your mind needs to shift into a different state to escape and refresh. **Rejuvenation is like a mini-vacation for your mind. It is the adult version of play.** It is an alternate way of "being" and "doing" that temporarily escapes both your Authentic and Synthetic expressions of existence so you can recharge.

AUTHENTIC PURPOSE

The identification of your **Life Theme** and your **Three Kinds of Self Expression** answers our original question, "Who are you?" Through the John Voris Method, I use this information to explore new questions about your authentic purpose:

- What is your social role and why?
- What is your Life Theme designed to express?
- What gives your Life Theme meaning?
- What gives you purpose?
- What gives you happiness?

You are a hero through your particular way of coming to the aid of people. This is your gift and it is driven by your **Life Theme.**

All of us need all four of the Universal Virtues regardless of our upbringing, opportunities, and physical attributes:

- If humans could not learn survival skills, find social cooperation, or change our environment through creative thought, we could not take care of our loved ones or ourselves. We would not know how to show compassion to others. (Love Virtue)
- If humans did not have the ability to find mutually beneficial symmetry in moral and ethical relationships among each other, society could not function as a whole and we could not survive. As it is, life gives us a sense of belonging. (Justice Virtue)
- If humans were not curious to learn about our environment, how to associate with others, or how to feed, clothe, or protect ourselves from the environment, we could not survive. As it is, life gives us meaning. (Wisdom Virtue)
- If humans did not have the motivation to act and change our environment or ourselves, we could not survive. Humans are the least prepared species on the planet for physical survival except for our ability to invent and create change. (Power Virtue)

With the John Voris Method, you can look to your inner circle and find how your **Life Theme** contributes to your circle of friends, lovers, relatives, and acquaintances.

How do you and your Life Theme hold the group together? We all come to the rescue of our intimate village. Your Authentic Purpose describes your capacity and ability to contribute for the good of the world.

REAL CHANGES TO REAL LIVES

Throughout this book, I will share case studies, stories of real people with whom I have worked who faced challenging issues. Through my assessment of and collaboration with these clients, I changed their lives. These stories are gathered from my many years of helping people. I share them to help illustrate the value of the Life Theme information in the context of real-life situations for real people.

DISCOVERING YOUR AUTHENTIC IDENTITY WILL CHANGE YOUR LIFE

Discovering your **Life Theme** using the John Voris Method can be a deeply liberating experience. Major positive changes have occurred in the lives of those with whom I've worked using the John Voris Method. When you sign up to work with me, you too can use this methodology and self-discovery for incredible self-acceptance, self-esteem, self-validation, and self-respect, generating gigantic epiphanies in the realms of your relationship and career.

2. The Four Life Themes

Congratulations! By reading this book, you're going to learn who you really are beneath your personality. To truly understand yourself, you need to remember that there are Four Life Themes. These Life Themes are the timeless, universal virtues essential to the human condition we introduced in the previous section of this book: **Love, Justice, Wisdom,** and **Power.**

These labels do not confine us nor box us in. They define our fundamental motivation in life beyond our human personalities. Who we truly are cannot confine us; on the contrary, knowing ourselves Authentically is what sets us free.

A word of caution: don't be fooled by the simplicity of the four Universal Virtues! There can be a lot of power in four elements. (Please see the Definitions Section for more information about the Power of Four.) It doesn't need to be complicated in order to be useful. A shift in perspective is often the most effective catalyst for positive change. Seeing yourself and others authentically, perhaps for the very first time, is a tremendously validating experience for you and for them. For most who encounter this material, it is quite literally life changing.

Our power is found in our Authentic potential before life had a chance to impose the expectations of others upon us; forcing the dreams of others to hinder our unique path to contentment, moments of joy, and success. Our shared world tends to push us toward social conformity to the point where we may not truly know who we are as individuals. Through the insight contained within these pages, may you begin a truly remarkable journey of self-discovery. Use this knowledge to enhance your life and the lives of others around you.

Research shows a major cause of anxiety in life occurs when we strive to conform to the expectations of others to the detriment of our own authentic well-being. We often suppress our opinions and even knowledge if we feel such expression may cause others discomfort, conflict or worse—anger.

SECTION II
LEARNING THE LIFE THEMES

3. Love: Advocates of Humanity

"The sole meaning of life is to serve humanity."
   –Leo Nikolayevich Tolstoy

"As far as we can discern, the sole purpose of human existence is to kindle a light in the darkness of mere being."
   – Carl Jung

"Compassion is a foundation for sharing our aliveness and building a more humane world."
   –Martin Lowenthal

The Love Domain

If your Life Theme is Love you possess a keen awareness of the needs of self and others. You intuitively seek well-being. You see yourself within others and you identify with them more easily than the other Life Themes do. Love finds its expression and purpose through you as an advocate and champion of the people.

Compared to the other Life Themes, Love People more easily sympathize (feel) and often empathize with (emotion) the pain that other people experience. They may choose to advocate for the wants and desires of all of humanity, either through their own singular voice, or though joining forces with others in groups.

The Love Person may be compelled to rescue others from their pain and suffering. Love People are likely to focus on those in need, and will attempt to alleviate their discomfort, in some fashion: listening to them, being with them, providing comfort, or playing the role of advocate by telling others about their suffering. This also applies to the Love Person's own situation: they may be pre-occupied with their own well-being and usually will freely communicate this to others.

In the larger scheme of things, Love People are motivated to improve the well-being of people. They see the world through the lens of compassion and empathy. In the Love Person's worldview, everyone should check in with one another and lend a hand if needed. Most Love People prefer to be part of a team, family unit, community, or some other group nurturing environment.

The Love Person is a humanitarian. Well-being is the focus and motivation behind everything that the Love person does or doesn't do, whether it's the well-being of self, of other people, or of the well-being of animals, plants and the environment.

As with all the Life Themes, finding lack of their Life Theme expression is a motivating force. We are always unconsciously motivated by our psychological desire for symmetry. For Love People, that means a lack of love, or lack of well-being—in any situation—is the primary motivator. It is not necessarily up to the Love Person to always remedy the situation, but it is their

Authentic role to bring this lack of Love to the attention of others.

Love People are well-suited to careers or volunteer opportunities that require service to others. To serve people is considered the greatest honor, for it moves humanity forward toward its capacity for self-realization.

Life Through the LOVE Lens

It's important to clarify that being a Love Person does not mean you have no Power, Wisdom or Justice!

Every person embodies and experiences all Four of the Universal Virtues with each one contributing toward achieving our goals. But your Life Theme provides the overall direction and the motivation for how you experience them.

With Love as your Life Theme, you are looking at Wisdom, Justice and Power through the lens of Love. *Love seeks Justice, Wisdom, and Power* **in order to** *express Love. Love seeks Love* **for the sake of** *Love.* (This is one method to separate the Life Theme from the function of our four Universal Virtues.) The way in which you experience Wisdom, Justice and Power is influenced by your desire for well-being. These three become reasons or tools for the Love Theme to use when needed. However, your Love Theme is an authentic state of being and expresses Love for its own sake without reason enabling your keen awareness of any lack of well-being.

A Love Theme would be a good kindergarten teacher who loves children and enjoys watching their young minds learn. This teacher doesn't not need a reason to love children, it is just natural. However, **in order to** be in the position to teach, years of Wisdom must first be accumulated usually in the form of a college degree and teaching credentials. **In order to** show student progress, the teacher must be in Action and develop students' activities to practice what they have learned. The teacher will then design a curriculum **in order to** generate a fair and just future society

The Love Person's Approach to Wisdom

Wisdom is the desire for knowledge. Love People maintain a focus on well-being. Keep in mind such well-being may apply to self or others.

If there is a conflict between doing what feels comfortable and stopping to gather more information, the Love Person will choose the former. That is, provided it does not conflict with other more important priorities. In other words, the Love Person's concern for well-being outweighs and/or overrides the desire for deeper knowledge whenever these two virtues are in conflict.

The Love Person's Approach to Justice

Love People feel very strongly about what is unjust when people's well-being is threatened. When it comes to societal matters and relationships, the Love Person will promote ideas, policies or legislation that increases well-being. They will also strongly oppose any impediments to people's well-being using ideas, policies or legislation.

The Love Person's Approach to Power

Power is a drive to act. Love People maintain a focus on human well-being, so the action that is taken or not taken is governed by the potential impact on well-being (again, it may be his or her own well-being, the well-being of other people, pets, environment, etc.).

Love People wish to avoid taking any action that could diminish well-being. Remember, the well-being may be his or her own, that of people close to him or her, that of humanity on the whole, or non-human (such as plants, animals, the environment, etc.).

The Love Person is acutely tuned in to those various instances of diminished well-being, and will readily communicate their sensibilities and findings to those who do take action.

Love People embrace Power as a tool to personally contribute to their well-being or the well-being of others. Mostly, Love People are seen to embody the "power of love," for example, through care-giving and service-oriented vocational and family roles. A Love Person who is an artist may take action in creating art that advocates for well-being or publicizes its lack.

LOVE: The Pitfalls of Projection

For the Love Person, projection takes the form of assuming that others would, could, will or should care about well-being as their primary concern.

Frustration occurs when others lack sympathy or empathy for anyone who is abused, enduring pain, or suffering on any level. The Love Person views this unsympathetic person as inconsiderate at best, and as a cruel victimizer at worst. Anyone who causes struggle in the lives of others, regardless of the reason, is to be avoided.

Contentment occurs when everyone meets or exceeds the Love Person's expectations of compassion. When others demonstrate compassionate and considerate behavior driven by a sense of humanity, then respect from Love People is almost guaranteed. When others listen openly and honor the Love Person's needs and desires, the Love Person feels supported, nurtured, heard and... loved.

The Love Person is drawn to situations that lack Love so they can fill that lack. For them, feeling the frustration of that lack, motivates them to the situation resulting in Contentment, once remedied. However, the cycle repeats endlessly, as it is the Authentic role of the Love Person to tune into situations where Love is lacking, and report on this to others.

As is true with all the Life Themes, contentment with other people occurs when you accept the Themes of others for what they are. The Love Person can learn to accept that other people are not necessarily focused on well-being, but that these other Themes still have an important role in our collective existence.

The LOVE Person's Strengths

- Appreciation and cheerfulness
- Compassion, thoughtfulness and caring for others
- Kind, thoughtful, and forgiving nature
- Transparency and realness
- Sensitive and empathetic to other's feelings
- Helpful, loyal, trusting and supportive of others

Everyone has strengths and challenges. The Love Person's strong suit is their ability to care deeply. Where would society be without our Love People?

The caring, compassionate, kind and thoughtful Love Person demonstrates these qualities to the other Life Themes, reminding us all of the importance of Love.

The LOVE Person's Challenges

- Being overly trusting of others
- Being extremely open and vulnerable
- Being overly dependent on others
- Being subservient to the self-esteem of others
- Being averse to taking on the responsibility of others

- Being prone to emotional drama

For Love People, their wants and desires are tethered to the dynamics of one motivation: to express and promote compassion, empathy, sympathy and caring, and to feel the same in return.

It's a noble purpose, one that greatly benefits the entire human race. The Love Person is here to remind us of our humanity in all its frailty, contradiction, beauty and depth. The love person is here to continually re-direct our efforts toward important matters of the heart.

Because of this focus, the Love Person can be plagued by undue sacrifices. They tend to give too much because they care so much. They may suffer from low self-esteem as they place greater value on the well-being of others.

A Love Person can be reluctant to take on responsibility because of potentially causing distress or suffering to others. A position of authority is a tricky thing for the Love Person to hold. This conflict appears in many facets of life. The Love Person often resorts to people-pleasing behavior to avoid conflict.

Other Life Themes may at times regard a Love Person's choices as irrational even though the Love Person is unlikely to regret his/her own decisions. Well-being is the great guiding principle, and all else is secondary for Love People. Staying within his or her integrity and honoring feelings is paramount. Everything else amounts to the minor details of this life.

With recognizing your Life Theme as Love, you can begin to release any negative self-judgment and appreciate your special purpose. Later in the book, you'll find more insights about your relationships with the other Life Themes.

John's Case Study: PLAYING THE NUMBERS

Barbara was a Love Theme client. As with most Love Themes, she was able to empathize with others easily. As you can imagine, she was very sensitive to how others expressed their feelings toward her in her personal and business life.

Barbara's dad owned a car dealership. When she was a high school junior, he hired her for part-time work in the accounting department as an assistant to earn money and get working experience. While she appreciated the opportunity, she found the work far too stressful.

After graduation, she left her home town for college and found another job in accounting. She was told it was the only job for which she was qualified. She knew she would be stepping into another stressful position but her work experience dominated her field of job choices.

Her major in college was Social Sciences. She had hopes of finding a career as a Social Worker. She always felt accomplished when helping others and wanted to help the disadvantaged link with social programs to ease their financial difficulties. After graduating from college, however, she found it difficult finding openings for social work. She moved on to another, now full-time, job in a car dealership accounting department.

When she came to me, her main issue was "...not letting so much bother me or stress me out. I want to find what makes me happy."

Barbara answered phones, cashiered, performed payroll duties, processed dealer trades, took care of payables/receivables, processed car sales documentations, and more. She was always there to help anyone who needed help, from the owner and the sales staff to the customers. She found joy in making others happy and getting what they wanted. She enjoyed having the department work like a family helping each other. She felt she was empowering others by giving them information they needed.

While Barbara prided herself as a nurturer, she was consistently stuck in the middle by demands to rush paperwork to completion, by debates with the sales staff about their commission checks, and by constant pressure from the owner for financial updates.

After our assessment, Barbara learned, as is typical for Love Themes, working with numbers was peaceful and had important meaning in her life. For Barbara, mathematics offered a specific repeatable method not up for debate. Math was dependable, reliable, and exact. However, in this dealership, the rules on which circumstances were needed to apply which numbers were not always clear-cut, especially when it came to who got commissions and at what percentages. Rather than being acknowledged for helping others in a manner Barbara thought was "above and beyond", her co-workers regarded her as simply doing her job. Barbara learned she was sensitive to the fact her authentic identity went without acknowledgement.

It frequently happens people stay in their first job far too long, and this had happened to Barbara. She now knew how the dealership industry functioned and it was not going to get better. She gave her two weeks' notice and secured a part-time job as a bookkeeper in a local department store. She used her extra time in securing a job as a Social Worker. Less than two months later, Barbara finally found what she needed: peaceful predictable surroundings. And that is what made her happy.

4. Justice: Arbiters of Humanity

"All things come into being by conflict of opposites."
   –Heraclitus

"...[o]nly justice, fairness, consideration and cooperation can finally lead men to the dawn of eternal peace."
   –Dwight D. Eisenhower

"It is the harmony of the diverse parts, their symmetry, their happy balance; in a word it is all that introduces order, all that gives unity, that permits us to see clearly and to comprehend at once both the ensemble and the details."
   –Henri Poincare

The Justice Domain

The Justice Virtue always has a dual purpose and interest. If Justice is your Life Theme, you possess an intuitive awareness of what is fair, right and good and can balance between fact and sentiment. Justice finds its expression and purpose through you in two ways. First, abstractly, as an arbiter and negotiator, guiding others toward the ideas of excellence and integrity. Second, physically, as an artist or engineer seeking symmetry and harmony through the art of creating.

We are all aware for every positive there is a negative, for every right there is a wrong. We all know we are confronted with:

- The one and the many
- The potential and the actual
- The united and the separated
- The conscious and the unconscious
- The authentic and the artificial
- The universal and the particular
- The smooth and the rough
- The straight and the curved

The list is endless. We all understand the meaning of these polarities and how to recognize them, just as we know and recognize the difference between compassion and knowledge in our daily lives. However, Justice People live with these distinctions every day and by the hour. Their lives are a journey of seeking symmetry and harmony:

- An architect brings function and aesthetics
- A landscape artist brings together nature and human imagination
- A chef finds balance to ingredients, temperature and time.
- A negotiator finds harmony between two in conflict
- An editor seeks symmetry between the author and the world

For the Justice Theme, these careers are natural and are where their individual unique talents are on display. For all careers and for all Life Themes, it's not just CAN you do the job but can you do it well, enjoy doing it with personal fulfillment. Unfortunately, people focus on what they CAN do and fail to see what they should be doing.

The Justice Life Theme is unique in that it represents a combination of two of the other universal virtues: Love plus Wisdom. Finding balance in human affairs requires empathy to want to help others and knowledge to bring about positive change. The particular ratio of Love to Wisdom varies from one Justice Person to the next. It is just as common for a Justice Person to express 80% Wisdom and 20% Love, as it is to express 80% Love and 20% Wisdom. Any mix will generate healthy achievements in life.

Justice Life Theme search for equilibrium between dual or opposing forces: light vs. dark, good vs. bad, pros and cons. This is an innate ability in all of us but what Justice People master.

As a Justice Person, you are continually striving for greater balance and harmony in your personal life, within your emotions, your home, your family, your social circle, your career or field of interest, and in the larger society. You derive all meaning, purpose, understanding, direction and motivation from your very personalized belief system.

Justice People tend to be excellent sympathetic listeners, enabling them to negotiate, moderate, settle disputes or provide counsel to others. They can speak the Love Person and the Wisdom Person's language and act as a translator or bridge between the two worlds.

To most Justice People, the idea of "might makes right" or "majority rules" is a deplorable thing to be avoided or railed against. Individual well-being is important, but it's also necessary for the Justice person to temper this cause and remain reasonable by balancing it with Wisdom.

Justice People are often entrepreneurs because they can see what humans need and they have the knowledge to deliver what is needed. The key to an entrepreneurship lies in seeing the whole picture while striking a balance of options, opportunities, risks, and structure. The Justice Person is able to weigh these factors and create a new design of something better. They can be found in the legal profession because of their interest in social justice and intuitive understanding of balance.

Justice People can find joy in design and engineering positions because they understand symmetry and what perfection should look like. They have an intuitive understanding of boundaries and they understand how objects interact with one another. They enjoy putting pieces of a puzzle together.

This also applies to music. Justice People can be found in the music industry as its very existence relies on balance and harmony, on the symmetry of sound and rhythm.

Harmony and balance are the ultimate achievement.

Life through the JUSTICE Lens

It's important to clarify that being a Justice Person does not mean you have no Love, Wisdom, or Power!

Every person embodies and experiences all Four of the Universal Virtues. But your Life Theme provides the direction and the motivation for how you experience all four.

With Justice as your Life Theme, you are looking at Love, Wisdom, and Power through the lens of Justice. *Justice seeks Love, Wisdom, and Power* **in order to** *express Justice. Justice seeks Justice* **for the sake of** *Justice.*

The ways in which you experience Love, Wisdom, and Power are influenced by your desire for balance and fairness, and your keen awareness of any imbalance or injustice you perceive.

The Justice Person's Approach to Love

Love is a focus on human well-being, and Justice is the act of balancing well-being with Wisdom. The Justice Person determines why someone is deserving of love and what it means to be loved through the lens of this balancing act. It's a merit system that Justice follows in matters of Love, rather than the unconditional across-the-board style Love People usually demonstrate. Those deemed just and worthy will be loved and adored by the Justice Person. Those who act unjustly will be deplored or avoided by the Justice Person.

The Justice Person's Approach to Wisdom

Wisdom is a focus on knowing, and Justice is the act of balancing that need to know with a concern for human well-being.

The Justice Person will be curious to learn more about things he or she sees as good and right and just. Justice People desire knowledge that enables chaos to lessen and become more orderly. They want to know things that help them create more balance between immediate human needs and wise choices.

Often, a Justice Person speaks in duality. The wisdom gleaned has duality in it: this, but that. On the one hand... but on the other hand. This is Justice weighing Wisdom like an old-fashioned scale seeking balance with Love.

The Justice Person's Approach to Power

Power represents the drive to act. The Justice Person will take action if he or she determines the action will help achieve greater balance, harmony or rightness. If action seems to create more chaos and more imbalance, the Justice Person will refrain from or avoid taking action. Justice People use their personalized belief systems to determine if there are abuses of power, as well as determine who deserves to be empowered.

JUSTICE: The Pitfalls of Projection

It's only human to project one's own perspective onto others. We all do it routinely without even realizing it. Projection means that we assume others are just like us—they think like us, act like us, and want the same things for the same reasons as we do. Each theme is designed to generate a specific projection of the world that produces stability, happiness, and predictability.

Occasionally our projections are faulty and create confusion and unhappiness because we drape our themed-vision on a chaotic world. Chaos sometimes leaks past the veil we've made for ourselves to create the illusion of safety and predictability.

For the Justice Person, projection takes the form of assuming that others would, could, will or should care about "getting it right," whatever "it" may be (per the Justice Person's own definitions).

Frustration takes place when there is unfairness, disorder or incompetence present. Justice People are very aware of these types of negative influences and pick up on disorder more than the other Life Themes. Therefore, frustration occurs often.

Another form of frustration for the Justice Person is an occasional feeling of overwhelm because they always see the alternatives in any situation.

For example: if there is a large project that has to be worked on, the Justice Person will feel overwhelmed because they're always thinking in dualities; "either I do this or I do that", and can't make up their mind. Often this results in "analysis paralysis" and feeling stuck or inadequate.

One way to help when this happens is to describe the tasks of the project out loud. You can only say one word at a time and this helps to exclude alternate thoughts.

Another tool is when you design your future, create a singular plan that is executed in a fixed chronology and follow it to the exclusion of anything else. Leave it flexible for the unforeseeable but design your reaction to such contingencies.

Contentment

Contentment occurs when balance, harmony or rightness is achieved. Justice People are unavoidably attracted to imbalance in all its forms driving them toward restoring order and balance, forging mutual agreements, and finding harmonious resolutions.

In this way, the Justice Person continually seeks and finds new "projects" to get to work in balancing. Frustration and Contentment go hand in hand: Frustration with imbalance, Contentment in restoring balance. So the cycle continues.

As is true with all the Life Themes, contentment with other people occurs when you accept the Themes of others for what they are. The Justice Person can learn to accept that other people are not necessarily focused on rightness or fairness, but these other Themes still have an important role in our collective existence.

The JUSTICE Person's Strengths

- Striving for and embodying balance and harmony
- Able to manage and organize a lot of diversified input
- Can find patterns in everything
- Seeks fairness and the balance of power
- Resourceful
- Natural entrepreneurs

Where would society be without Justice People to fine-tune things and bring balance and fairness to our lives?

The JUSTICE Person's Challenges

- Trouble accepting compliments and giving them
- Fear of being wrong and harming others
- Perfectionism and constant re-tweaking
- Exhausted by so many alternatives
- Always trying to be right and avoid criticism
- Procrastination

- Can be passive aggressive

Justice People tend to hold a negative view of authority. They may complain about those in power, while being hesitant and disinterested in assuming a leadership role themselves, for fear of infringing on anyone's well-being. Generally, they are averse to politics because it often has more to do with connections and manipulation of public opinion than skills or qualifications. From the Justice Person's perspective, this is unjust, and politics is the probable cause of a lot of imbalance and unfairness within business, government, and social circles.

Justice People appreciate rules but strongly prefer that others self-regulate. The Justice Person prefers and desires stable, peaceful environments free of drama or other extreme emotional situations.

Justice People easily detect hypocrisy in others and have no problem calling others out when they perceive this "ultimate unfairness." A Justice Person's preoccupation with what is "fair" and "not fair" may at times distort their perception. They may detect imbalance where, objectively, there is none.

Those driven by Justice can easily fall into "analysis paralysis" as they endlessly compare pros and cons of an issue. The Justice Person is often cautious when making decisions for fear of making the wrong choice by missing an alternate position. Others may interpret this as a lack of personal drive, fickleness, indecisiveness, or apathy.

Justice People tend to be highly trusting and loyal to others. They may get sucked into situations and relationships that are less than advantageous, or even detrimental to their own well-being. Because the Justice Person usually exhibits a high degree of tolerance and patience, others may pick up on this and attempt to take advantage. Friends and family may pressure them to stop being a "pushover." They are typically very trusting of individuals but distrusting of social systems that lack human warmth and empathy. The Justice Person is predisposed to being a workaholic and having perfectionist tendencies in striving to "get it right."

Justice People are often careful with their emotions and feelings, ensuring they won't swing too far to one side or the other. They usually exhibit a good degree of modesty and amiability but may suffer from impaired self-esteem. The tendency to self-deprecate stems from a desire to avoid standing out or being perceived by others as an egotist or braggart. They prefer to be seen as someone living in the center of life. Most Justice People will readily take a stand on behalf of others, but are slow to defend themselves when the need arises.

If you are a Justice Person, you have doubtlessly found resonance in the preceding description. Recognizing your Life Theme as Justice, can you begin to release any self-judgment and appreciate your special purpose?

Later in the book, you'll find more insights about your relationships with the other Life Themes.

John's Case Study: SON'S SELF SABOTAGE

I worked with a family whose son had abused drugs, alcohol, and his body with scarification. He had attempted suicide. He was considered the "outsider". Things had become so bad, in fact, he was no longer allowed in the family's house.

The family didn't have much hope my assessment would make a difference, but they were desperate to try anything. I made it clear I am not a psychotherapist, but felt willing and able to help.

In assessing this troubled young man, I discovered he was a Justice Person and a "Radical Rescuer" who needed a victim to rescue. He wasn't able to get in touch with this inner need, partly due to the imposition of familial demands. With no one to rescue, he became his own victim.

This example shows the extreme people will go to in order to express their Authentic Identity. One will find one's victim to rescue or be rescued even at the risk of one's own physical well-being.

This information rang true and deep. Barriers began to melt away. I'll never forget how he and his mother sat in the parking lot outside my office for two hours afterward and just cried. The healing had begun.

The son showed vast behavioral improvement and became involved in a non-profit organization that assists people after tornadoes and floods here in the U.S. and abroad.

When you begin to know and live your Authentic Identity, positive changes—both big and small—are the result.

5. Wisdom: Teachers of Humanity

"If we do not plant knowledge when young, it will give us no shade when we are old."
 –**Lord Chesterfield**

"One's first step in wisdom is to question everything–and one's last is to come to terms with everything."
 –**Georg Christoph Lichtenberg**

"The beginning of wisdom is found in doubting; by doubting we come to the question, and by seeking we may come upon the truth."
 –**Pierre Abélard**

The Wisdom Domain

If Wisdom is your Life Theme, you possess a natural, deep desire to grasp knowledge. You are driven by a need to know–in order to exercise sound judgment in problem solving and goal attainment. Wisdom finds its expression and purpose through you as a teacher of the people.

The Wisdom Person's approach to problem solving is highly objective, and therefore far less likely to be concerned with the current state of any single individual emotion. The Wisdom

Person's pursuit of knowledge is relentless, bordering on compulsive, which others might perceive as obsessive.

Being a Wisdom Person does not mean you know all there is to know, or even everything about a certain topic. Nor does it mean you will always make the wisest decisions. Rather, it means you are **driven to know** what you feel is required, and you will continue to learn more and more until you are sufficiently satisfied only to be driven again.

Wisdom People are distinct from the other three Life Themes in that they separate wisdom from knowledge. Knowledge demands information and the accumulation of facts. Wisdom assesses these facts within a larger framework of understanding, discernment and experience.

When somebody asks a question of the Wisdom Person they are a "fount of knowledge" and often exceed the question itself. However, they would rather listen than talk so they can accumulate more knowledge.

Wisdom People excel in careers or social roles requiring extensive knowledge. The Wisdom Person is happiest when serving as an expert go-to person or resource for others. He or she is more than happy to take on all the research and knowledge acquisition for which others have neither the time nor the inclination.

Life through the WISDOM Lens

It's important to clarify that being a Wisdom Person does not mean you have no Love, Justice or Power!

Every person embodies and experiences all Four of the universal virtues. But your Life Theme provides the direction and the motivation for how you experience the other three.

With Wisdom as your Life Theme, you are looking at Love, Justice and Power through the lens of Wisdom. *Wisdom seeks Love, Justice, and Power **in order to** express Wisdom. Wisdom seeks Wisdom **for the sake of** Wisdom.*

The way in which you experience Love, Justice and Power is influenced by your desire to know, and by your disdain for a perceived lack of knowledge.

The Wisdom Person's Approach to Love

Love is a focus on individual and collective well-being. The Wisdom Person is driven by a need to know. Whereas the Love Person wants to know about things that enhance well-being, the Wisdom Person's well-being is enhanced by knowing things.

On a personal level, the Wisdom Person respects and bonds with those who are knowledgeable and/or who demonstrate an interest in knowledge or the desire to know.

The Wisdom Person's Approach to Justice

Wisdom People maintain a focus on knowing, therefore the Wisdom Person will tend to view things as being "just" if they contain true knowledge or contribute to greater knowing. Wisdom people judge others by what they should they have known, what they actually knew, and when they knew it.

True injustice is found when those deemed "guilty" were not aware of being in violation of any crime or inappropriate act. For example, if someone were to be accused of a crime they really didn't know was criminal or were, in fact, given information their act was not criminal, then charging that person with a crime would be a great injustice in the opinion of the Wisdom Person.

The Wisdom Person's Approach to Power

Power is a drive to act, and Wisdom People maintain a focus on knowing. It is through knowledge and therefore Wisdom, that Power is energized into action.

The Wisdom Person's desire to act is governed in three ways. First, does he or she already have sufficient knowledge? If not, further action is required. Second, to what degree will further action enhance knowledge? That is, the action taken must be sufficient to produce the desired result. Lastly, the Wisdom Person's sense of contribution is getting into action and teaching others.

It is important to the Wisdom Person that Power People must act from informed power. Otherwise, power will be deemed impotent, irrelevant, illogical or even dangerous. Wisdom people intuit Power People's need for a great deal of control. They also seek empowering information and admire those who possess it. That make the Wisdom People very valuable to the Power People.

WISDOM: The Pitfalls of Projection

Remember, projection means we assume others are just like us—they think like us, act like us, and want the same things for the same reasons as we do. Each theme is designed to generate a specific projection of the world to produce stability, happiness, and predictability.

For the Wisdom Person, projection takes the form of assuming that others would, could, will or should be fully knowledgeable—whether it's a personal matter or within the scope of his or her chosen profession. Wisdom People are extremely curious, so in projection they often make the assumption that everybody "wants to know."

Frustration results when others don't know when they should have known. For Wisdom, finding facts is expected and even demanded from others. It can also be frustrating if others are disinterested in what the Wisdom Person has to say, or withhold information that the Wisdom Person seeks.

Contentment occurs when everyone is meeting or exceeding the Wisdom Person's expectations of knowing. The

Wisdom Person generally admires people of knowledge, provided the quality of knowledge is equal to or greater than their own.

Wisdom People are ceaselessly drawn to learn more. Due to this inherent inquisitive and acquisitive nature, the Wisdom Person may often find him or herself to be the most well-informed person in the room. This is a situation bound to trigger frustration. Through interacting with others the Wisdom person quickly finds he or she is in another world of thought. They often feel isolated with no one being interested in anything they have to say.

As is true with all the Life Themes, contentment with other people occurs when you accept the Themes of others for what they are. The Wisdom Person can learn to accept other people are not necessarily focused on learning and knowing, but that these other Themes still have an important role in our collective existence.

As stated earlier, once the Wisdom Person finds the most success in accessing one method of knowing over the others, those remaining methods become less active. This explains much about the "absent minded professor."

The WISDOM Person's Strengths

- Curious and open-minded
- Able to process vast amounts of information
- Objective and discerning

- Patient and diligent
- Idealistic and embracing of ideals
- Clever and resourceful thinking ability

Everyone has strengths and challenges. The Wisdom Person's strong suit is their ability to learn, know, and transmit information to others who can use it.

Whether they are specialists or generalists, Wisdom People play an invaluable role for the rest of humanity as experts, resources, teachers and counselors. Where would society be without our Wisdom People reading boring books so others won't need to?

The WISDOM Person's Challenges

- Being seen as intrusive and overly inquisitive
- Overwhelming people with information
- Being insensitive to others
- Being arrogant or presumptuous
- Becoming suspicious of others

Because of their irresistible drive and burning need to know, Wisdom People can be perceived by others as nosey or invasive. At times they may overwhelm others with too much information.

This inquisitive behavior is so deep-seated sometimes Wisdom People find themselves asking too many questions about a subject. Wisdom People need to know everything right now, so "in the moment" a particular topic may seem riveting, but later on a Wisdom Person may realize they really are not interested or attached to that subject at all.

Wisdom People grow accustomed to boring topics and conversations because they're minds are so active and often someplace else. They train themselves to hide their real feelings of boredom during many conversations, social gatherings, and meetings. They are master illusionists as they often feign interest in the topic at hand.

The Wisdom Person may dismiss another person's ideas too readily by presumptuously concluding they already know where the conversation is going. A "been there, done that" attitude can sometimes make others feel their ideas and contributions are not heard or valued.

Making assumptions about the motives of others is a common occurrence in the mind of a Wisdom Person. While the Wisdom Person may possess a high degree of accuracy in leaps of logic, other people don't always appreciate this mental game.

The Wisdom Person's very nature is to doubt and question everything. This can lead to strained relationships in two different ways. First, the Wisdom Person may be perceived as cold and calculating. Secondly, the Wisdom Person runs the risk of becoming overly suspicious of other people.

But in the long run, all these interpersonal challenges are generally shrugged off, because the Wisdom Person's Authentic drive is to know, know, and know some more. Knowing makes a Wisdom Person happy, and everything else remains secondary.

If you are a Wisdom Person, you have doubtlessly found resonance in the preceding description. Recognizing your Life Theme as Wisdom, can you begin to release any self-judgment and appreciate your special purpose?

Later in the book, you'll find additional perspective on your relationships with the other Life Themes.

John's Case Study: AUTO ANGER MANAGEMENT
A young man who worked at a car dealership was having behavioral problems. He had physically assaulted someone on the premises. Fortunately for him, that car dealership was owned by his father, so he did not lose his job. However, changes needed to be made... and soon.

I did an assessment for him and discovered he was a Wisdom Person. He was surrounded by a particular subculture, which did not hold voluntary learning and education in high esteem. In order to fit in at work, socially, and even with his family, he had unknowingly suppressed his Authentic Life Theme. The result was his volatile anger.

Understanding his Life Theme was a validating experience for him. No one in his immediate environment had ever validated his innate thirst for knowledge. I instructed him to take ownership of his Wisdom Life Theme rather than try to hide it or downplay it. He took my advice. He began to openly read books of all kinds everywhere in his life, even at the car dealership during down time.

Interestingly, when he learned who he was and accepted himself as a Wisdom Person, others accepted him, too. He reported seeing others reading at work, bringing books from home or reading automotive information.

Most gratifying of all was having his wife tell me he was a changed man. He no longer drank too much, he stopped smoking, and came home early whenever possible to be with her and their children. She was elated and beyond grateful.

In this specific instance, this young man and I did not discuss his anger under the umbrella of "anger management". Rather, we addressed the causal factor of his anger. The proof it worked was in the results confirmed by his wife.

When one's Authentic Identity is smothered, ignored, or harmed in some way, anger is the result. Anger, a temporary emotion, can be the result of other factors in one's life. **If your one and only need is to express your Authentic Identity through objects, relationships, and events, and if you suppress that need, anger is the only possible initial outcome.**

6. Power: Leaders of Humanity

"*Do not wait to strike till the iron is hot; but make it hot by striking.*"
–William Butler Yeats

"*He who leads and no one follows is just taking a walk.*"
– Anonymous

"*The most common way people give up their power is by thinking they don't have any.*"
–Alice Walker

Power Domain

If Power is your Life Theme, you possess a need to act upon your thoughts and get into action. Empowerment finds its expression and purpose through you as a natural leader and agent of change.

For you, Power is a very personalized belief system from which you derive all meaning, purpose, understanding, direction and motivation. In fact, your entire existence is spent validating Power as the one and only belief system that truly matters.

Power People tend to assume that everyone should seek their own empowerment, and weakness should be avoided at all costs.

Power People naturally see the potential that exists all around us and are driven to create opportunities where advancement and positive changes can be made. These advancements can take many forms, such as goal achievement, character improvements or skill acquisition.

The Power Person can provide the means and circumstances for others to discover and use their inner strengths, thus enabling them to gain a greater sense of completeness and control over their own lives.

In realizing and cultivating his or her natural gifts and qualities, the Power Person can transfer this experience into advising, consulting and guiding others to achieve their own self-realization and mastery.

Power People easily detect weaknesses in systems, methods, processes, situations, and people. This is their natural inclination and gift since it enables them to quickly formulate solutions to overcome those weaknesses.

For the Power Person, life is all about empowering themselves and others. They skew their interpretation of events towards "What is weak or broken", and persistently ask themselves: "What must be achieved to bring about change?"

Their objective nature (a focus on the bigger picture rather than the needs of a solitary individual), as well as their strong sense of empowerment and need for progressive advancement, make Power People well-suited for careers that enable them to lead, direct, guide, consult or coach others.

Power People seek others as a conduit for their personal expression of Power. Power is transferred from a manager to a subordinate, for example, who then makes that change into a reality.

The Power Person does not need to recognize the feelings of others, especially if they are couched in excuses to avoid responsibility and progress.

Life through the POWER Lens

It's important to clarify that being a Power Person does not mean you have no Love, Wisdom or Justice!

Every person embodies and experiences all Four of the universal virtues. But your Life Theme provides the direction and the motivation for how you experience the other three.

With Power as your Life Theme, you are looking at Love, Wisdom, and Justice through the lens of Power. *Power seeks Love, Wisdom, and Justice* **in order to** *express Power. Power seeks Power* **for the sake of** *Power.*

The way in which you experience Love, Wisdom, and Justice is influenced by your desire to take action and affect change.

The Power Person's Approach to Love

Love is a focus on individual and collective well-being, and the Power Person is driven by a need to act. The Power Person expresses love through action, whether it is doing something for a loved one, or joining an active project that delivers loving care in supplies to needy persons.

Caring for people involves action, possibly pragmatic changes, and responsibility but any change needs to be practical and effective. There is an outer demonstration of Love, as the Power Person is not inclined to sit around and just talk about feelings.

The Power Person's Approach to Wisdom

Wisdom is the desire for knowledge. Power People maintain a focus on action. Therefore, the Power Person's desire for knowledge is motivated by the underlying immutable desire for making things happen. Power also tends to be responsible for issues far beyond what's reasonable and feeds off of responsibility.

A Power Person will be interested or disinterested in information at hand, depending on whether it seems relevant to taking action. A Power Person will possess a desire to know more about anything they perceive will contribute to achieving their goals, whatever those goals may be. If information has seemingly nothing to do with making something happen or correcting a problem, a Power Person is likely to become disinterested.

The Power Person's Approach to Justice

Power is a drive to act and make things happen. To the Power Person, getting results is valued highly, so injustice is attributed to the presence of weakness. Achieving goals and affecting change is justified through what is good, and right. "The end justifies the means" and "all is fair in love in war" are expressions of Power.

Leadership is a Power Person's strong suit, whether the group being led is a family, a social group, a corporation, or a nation. Goals may be big or small, altruistic or not, but justice is served when accomplishments are achieved.

POWER: The Pitfalls of Projection

It's only human to project one's own perspective onto others. We all do it routinely without even realizing it. Projection means that we assume others are just like us: they think like us; act like us; and want the same things for the same reasons as we do. Each theme is designed to generate a specific projection of the world to produce personal stability, happiness, and predictability.

Occasionally our projections are faulty and create confusion and unhappiness. We drape our themed-vision on a chaotic world and that chaos sometimes leaks past the veil we created for ourselves to create the illusion of safety and predictability.

Power People are more than willing to be disliked because they live in the domain of Action. They know others will not always agree with the actions they propose and this occurs habitually. They are also driven by objective information and naturally view being in action far more important than the non-action of others. Leaders have to be in a position where they can't afford to care about the opinions of others.

For the Power Person, projection takes the form of assuming that others would, could, will or should take action on whatever issue is at hand—whatever can or should be done. Power People believe that weakness should be avoided at all costs, and in projection, they may expect other people to behave this way and hold this same belief.

Frustration

For them, frustration takes the form of someone complaining but not being willing to do anything about the situation—due to laziness, disempowerment or a strong belief in victimhood.

Frustration also occurs temporarily when the Power Person is somehow blocked from taking action when he or she knows action will be effective. This is especially true if the other person is perceived as not doing their job.

Contentment

Contentment occurs when everyone is empowered and doing what they need to do. The Power Person admires people who are not overly emotional and who possess the required knowledge the Power Person can use to take action.

As is true with all the Life Themes, contentment with other people occurs when you accept the Themes of others for what they are. The Power Person can learn to accept that other people are not necessarily focused on getting things done, but these other Themes still have an important role in our collective existence.

The POWER Person's Strengths

- Willingness to step in and actively take charge
- Belief in personal empowerment
- Enjoys challenges and competition
- Leadership ability
- Pragmatic, objective approach to problem-solving
- Has vast reserves of energy
- Willingness to be hyper responsible

Since they naturally see all the positive potential that being empowered can bring to someone's life, they often encourage others to realize this potential.

Power People move others past comfort zones offering a list of necessary actions and the vision of what real advancement looks like. However, these are all constructs the Power Person makes up and may not truly represent what is best for the other person, especially if their Life Theme is not Power.

Power People are natural leaders and the real "change agents" in social groups and business. Through the use of strong guidance they move the less assertive past their own perceived limitations to take bold and immediate action. Without Power individuals, organizations, and communities would remain static.

Authentic leaders generate an environment of meaning into which they and staff members are empowered through collaboration, giving purpose to their collective Authentic expression. Leaders are then able to move others from learning "to do" and performing a role, to a state of being that is accessible to all.

The POWER Person's Challenges

- Being seen as uncaring and insensitive to others
- Being seen as selfish and self-serving
- Being forceful, bossy, or pushy causing others to be resentful and possibly sabotaging efforts
- Knowing when to push and when not to push

The Power Person attempts to persuade those in need of empowerment that real benefits are to be had if they simply press onward and push past any imagined struggles, inconveniences, or other self-limiting beliefs.

Power People tend to feel strongly that if an individual finds themselves in a weakened state, that person must take prompt action to change themselves, their circumstances or both. But the Power Person may overestimate the other person's capacity for that type and kind of self-empowerment, thus causing conflict and a termination of the relationship.

More sensitive individuals may find a Power Person's strong, direct style to be overwhelming or intimidating. Out of pressure, they may agree to make changes, but without sincere intention or follow-through. When Power People come to this realization, they may feel frustrated, betrayed or perhaps a bit disempowered themselves.

If you are a Power Person, you have doubtlessly found resonance in the preceding description. Recognizing your Life Theme as Power, can you begin to release any negative self-judgment and appreciate your special purpose? Without expression of Power nothing would ever get done.

In the next section, you'll find more insights about your relationships with the other Life Themes.

John's Case Study: WHO'S THE BOSS?
As a member of a philanthropic organization, I frequently meet with other board members. In one meeting with the other

office holders, the discussion moved to why the group was not following the stipulated event guidelines. All five of our members held four-year college degrees, and altogether we represented decades of business experience. However, after 30 minutes of discussion, the president pointed out we had not made a single decision.

It occurred to me why this occurred. I realized within our group of board members, none of us had a Power Life Theme. Not only did we lack a member with the Power Theme, but none of us felt comfortable stepping into the Power Domain, either. As a result, even though we had education, training, business acumen, self-confidence and life experience, the group lacked leadership.

In this situation, not much ever got done in a timely manner. The club suffered for it. We would have welcomed any twenty-year-old with a Power Life Theme to step in to run the show.

SECTION III
LEARNING HOW THE LIFE THEMES INTERACT

7. Interaction

"I think for any relationship to be successful, there needs to be loving communication, appreciation, and understanding."
   –Miranda Kerr

"The leader's job is not to do the work for others, it's to help others figure out how to do it themselves, to get things done, and to succeed beyond what they thought possible."
   –Simon Sinek

"In every community, there is work to be done. In every nation, there are wounds to heal. In every heart, there is the power to do it."
   –Marianne Williamson

The Four Life Themes work in concert together in society. Everyone has an important role. We could not function without all four Life Themes. Here is an imagined template to illustrate their thematic interconnectedness:

- A Love Person turns on the faucet and discovers the water flowing out of it is brown and polluted. The Love Person's role is to notice when Love or well-being is lacking, and communicate this to others. So the Love Person turns to a Justice Person and exclaims this urgent, horrible situation.
- The Justice Person is an arbiter or negotiator between

Love and Wisdom. They empathize easily with others and gather enough information to come to the aid of those harmed. They weigh and analyze the strength of the harm done against the efficacy of reasonable solutions justifying their recommendations. The Justice Person responds to the Love Person's outcry about the water by listening with compassion and analyzing the complaint. It is concluded there is justification. The Justice Person then contacts the Wisdom person.

- The Wisdom Person becomes expert on water quality issues, and provides the needed information. The Wisdom person contacts those in Power and offers sufficient information for the correct Action to take place.
- The Power Person steps in to remedy the situation, taking swift action in accordance with the Wisdom Person's recommendations. Then the Power Person checks in with the Love Person to assure the problem has been solved. With the water quality restored, the Love Person is content again. And so it goes. The cycle recurs in another situation.

On an individual level, the following exemplifies how we all engage with the Four Virtues in daily life:

Kim goes to her faucet and sees dark rusty looking water coming out of the tap. She naturally **cares** for the health of those in the home. She **knows** water should be clear. Immediately she thinks "this is **not right**". She gets into **action**, calls the local water company and registers her complaint.

Essential Motivating Factors for Life Themes

All Life Themes seek out the opposite condition of what their Life Theme offers. Motivation requires tension between opposite conditions such to have and to not have. For a love theme to be motivated, he or she must be aware that love is missing and can be addressed. For Justice, Wisdom and Power the motivating pattern is the same.

- **Love Life Theme People** seek out those in need of care.
- **Wisdom Life Theme People** seek out the unknowing to teach them
- **Justice Life Theme People** seeks out imbalance and chaos that needs to be restored to balance.
- **Power Life Theme People** seek out those who need change through empowerment.

Universal Projection

It's only human to project one's own perspective onto others. We assume others have the same amount of empathy with others as we do. We assume others have the same intensity of empathy with others including the same kind and type of empathy and for the same reasons.

Here is how people with each Life Theme universally projects their perspective onto others:

- **Love Life Theme** people assume others care for people as they do.
- **Wisdom Life Theme** people assume others have the same need to know as they do.
- **Justice Life Theme** people assume others have the same need for social fairness and symmetry as they do.
- **Power Life Theme** people assume others have the same need for personal empowerment as they do.

All of us make these projections routinely without even realizing it. Each Life Theme is designed to generate a specific projection onto the world to produce stability, happiness, and predictability for that Life Theme.

Occasionally our projections are faulty and create confusion and unhappiness. We all drape our Themed-vision on a chaotic world to capture understanding. However, sometimes that chaos leaks past the veil we created for ourselves and our illusion of safety breaks down.

Here are a few examples of how this breakdown can occur:

- We may find ourselves protecting the wrong person or the wrong cause
- We may find ourselves promoting the wrong idea for the wrong reasons
- We may find ourselves promoting what is ultimately the unfair
- We may find ourselves empowering the corporate tyrant

The Harmony and Expression of Authentic Energy

While each of the Universal Virtues—Love, Justice, Wisdom and Power—applies to everyone, only one of the Universal Virtues is dominant in all of us. This is known as your Life Theme.

All of us need all four of the Universal Virtues regardless of upbringing, opportunities, and physical attributes.

Every person embodies and experiences all four of the Universal Virtues. But your Life Theme provides the direction and the motivation for how you experience the other three.

When you know your dominant Life Theme, you simultaneously know you also possess each of the other three Life Themes to varying degrees. The contribution of one of those three will be significantly less than the other two. You'll be dominant in the expression of one Universal Virtue and weak in the expression of another. This lesser expression is the antithesis of the dominant Universal Virtue.

So, typically, it is normal and natural for:

- **Love Life Theme** people occasionally feel they lack Wisdom
- **Wisdom Life Theme** people occasionally feel they lack Justice
- **Justice Life Theme** people occasionally feel they lack

Power
- **Power Life Theme** people occasionally feel they lack Love

Strong Convictions

Have you ever found yourself arguing based on your beliefs, even when it wasn't popular for you to do so? When people of each Life Theme sense their Life Theme is being threatened, they are willing to stand up for themselves, despite the circumstances. Notice when you are **willing to be disliked**, you have a high degree of conviction and confidence, supported directly by your Life Theme.

- **Love Life Theme** people argue when they sense someone is being hurt
- **Wisdom Life Theme** people argue when they sense ignorance
- **Justice Life Theme** people argue when they sense unfairness
- **Power Life Theme** people argue when they sense weakness

Personal Relationships

When it comes to personal relationships, the Life Themes relate to one another quite differently than they do in the larger framework of humanity and society.

In social gatherings **without** well-defined goals, you will find this pattern: Love and Justice People tend to gravitate toward each other, while Wisdom and Power People group together.

In situations **with** well-defined stated goals, people with the same Life Theme tend to work well together: Love People working well with other Love People, Justice People with other Justice people and so on.

8. Love and Wisdom Interaction

Love People want to feel wise, however, they will only seek wisdom if it serves the purpose of creating comfort, help and well-being for others and themselves.

Wisdom People want to feel fair and just, however, they lack the sufficient amount of the love component comprising Justice, which gives empathy, and an overabundance of Wisdom tilting their view to extremes. After all, the Wisdom People's true gift is their ability to focus on the intellectual side and ignore the emotional, causing an imbalance in perception.

A Love Person and a Wisdom Person

Knowledge is an important component in the decision-making process for Love People to ensure the well-being of themselves and others. Love People can appreciate data, information and logic; however, compassion, empathy and emotions dominate their intentions.

Love People will rise in protest when knowledge and information are used to justify suffering. For them, suffering is the signal that information is missing or that knowledge is being withheld. This is likely to cause conflict.

Love's Frustration with Wisdom

The Love Person may find the Wisdom Person to be cold, calculating, uncaring, and unduly focused upon things that don't matter.

Love's Contentment with Wisdom

When the Wisdom Person uses knowledge to enhance well-being (of the Love Person or others), the Love Person finds value and purpose in the information offered.

Love People are eager for others to offer new ways to combat suffering in the world, so when the Wisdom Person uses knowledge in this fashion, these two will join forces harmoniously.

A Wisdom Person and a Love Person

Compassion for others is based on knowing the full circumstances before any action is taken. Wisdom people tend to help those who help themselves. If the needy person is simply a lifelong victim, then support will not be forthcoming from the Wisdom Person. If, on the other hand, that person was self-sufficient at one point but fell on hard times, a Wisdom Person will be more than generous.

Wisdom's Frustration with Love

The Wisdom Person can become frustrated because the Love Person may seem illogical and unnecessarily emotional.

They can be unwilling or unable to see the important details or the bigger picture. They certainly dismiss any justification for others to be harmed. There must always be a better way.

Wisdom's Contentment with Love

The Wisdom Person can be content when realizing Love People provide important information to keep all of us focused on the meaning and purpose we create in life for ourselves and others. A Wisdom Person will be content with the Love person when it comes to those he or she cares about. A good example would be those in the health care business. A Wisdom person will know their loved one will be cared for.

Love People are also the first to grasp the pain of others and to notice the need for change. They inform the rest of us if problem-solving techniques are working or not. Love People provide feedback to let us know if we are doing a good job. They also provide Love, which the Wisdom Person appreciates, as does everyone.

9. Love and Justice Interaction

Because the Justice Theme consists of part Love and part Wisdom, a Justice Person finds strong kinship with a Love Person. It is very common to see pairings of Love People with Justice People.

This is because **Justice People** receive a lot of love from Love People in the form of emotions, feelings, and empathic connections which makes them feel good.

Love People receive wisdom from Justice People in addition to warm feelings and empathic connections which both come from the Justice Person's Love portion.

A Love Person and a Justice Person

Fairness is based on the need to counter the negative feelings and emotions of those being hurt. If someone is suffering from distress or anxiety, there is obviously an imbalance which must be corrected. When someone is placed at a disadvantage, Justice is served when intervention occurs and the issue is resolved.

Love's Frustration with Justice

Justice People often take too long to make pain-relieving decisions, and the reasons for delay may be faulty and harmful. The Love Person may find the Justice Person to be overly analytical, cold and uncaring, downright mean, perfectionist, or workaholic.

Love's Contentment with Justice

Justice People are empathetic and can usually see the passion that drives the Love Person. The Justice Person shares the Love Person's desire to avoid struggle, but also offers the Love Person an ability to design a fair resolution. The Love Person appreciates being heard, and the fact that the Justice Person's skills and strengths bring order and stability to the table.

A Justice Person and a Love Person

Because the Justice Person doesn't have 100% Love in their make-up, they need the emotional connection that a Love Person can offer.

Love People give empathy and heartfelt compassion. This provides a Justice Person with a sense of trust and acceptance no other Theme can give.

Justice's Frustration with Love

Since the Justice Person is compelled to always bring in the opposing view, they can come into conflict with a Love Person's disinterest in objective reasoning if it means suffering will persist. The Justice Person may find the Love Person to be overly emotional, one-sided or illogical. Drama is upsetting to the harmony-seeking Justice Person.

Love People may urgently and impatiently press a Justice person into taking humanitarian action before he or she has accurately weighed the situation, but rash or unjust decisions may result in guilt, shame, self-criticism, or regret.

Justice's Contentment with Love

The Love Person brings Love and perhaps levity and fun into a Justice Person's life. The Justice Person is empathetic and identifies well with the Love Person's passions. The Justice Person is able to give structure and balance to these passions. When balance is achieved, a sense of serenity and peace can prevail in the relationship

Case Study: HAPPY SPOUSE, HAPPY HOUSE
I worked with a couple experiencing bumps in the road of their married life. He felt she was distant, cold, and unfeeling. She felt he complained all the time and wasn't making rational sense.

If you've read through the book this far, you might guess he is a Love Person and she is a Justice Person. This information was

incredibly validating to them. It even triggered some laughter when they realized their own and each other's Life Theme.

Knowing the innate qualities of Love and Justice doesn't necessarily change behaviors, but it validates each person as being okay and not necessarily needing to change. These two people had a new clarity from which they could decide to make changes, if they wished. The important thing was they saw the value in their differences.

They understood why they were drawn to one another and how each other's strengths were a compliment. For example, the wife takes care of their finances and practical matters while her husband cooks delicious meals with Love. As a Justice Person, she keeps their life out of chaos, and as a Love Person, he lightens her up and makes sure they're still having fun. The differences are now something to laugh about rather than fodder to contemplate divorce.

10. Love and Power Interaction

Power People are all about action and they announce the actions needed to be done. If a Love Person agrees with the Power Person's agenda, then all is well. Ultimately, the Power People need Love People to serve the agenda.

Love People need Power People to offer structure, rules, and empowerment.

However, great conflict ensues if the Love Person feels an abuse of Power or oppression by a Power Person. In this instance, a Love Person will try to stop the efforts of a Power Person.

When a Love Person disagrees with a Power Person's plan for action it is perceived as an attempt to challenge the identity of the Power Person whose lifeblood is the expression of their freedom to act and build.

When these two Life Themes work together, mountains can be moved. However, when conflict appears, the clashes can be unyielding.

The best possibility is when they have a shared goal for what they value.

A Love Person and a Power Person

Love People tend to view Power as a means to control others. A Love Person may assume a position of power only if it can be used to promote well-being. However, they often find difficulty in administering leadership because they do not want to be the source of hardship for anyone. How can Love knowingly cause conflict and pain? In fact, spouses will often overlook abuse because they don't want to make the other person upset.

Love's Frustration with Power

The Love Person may find the Power Person to be cold, insensitive, uncaring, self-serving, domineering, and even deeply narcissistic. Love People find it intolerable when someone wields Power and lacks compassion.

Love's Contentment with Power: When Power is put to use in alleviating pain and discomfort or maintaining acceptable levels of compassion, the Love Person will embrace the Power Person with unswerving loyalty and devotion.

In larger society, this occurs with leaders who promise to bring positive change, replacing misery and discontent. They gain devoted Love People as followers. This is the reason political revolutions often succeed.

A Power Person and a Love Person

Power People often seem emotionless and cold to Love People. After all, Power People are usually embroiled in objective reality while Love People are seeking emotional empathy. Due to their practical attitude, Power People rarely consider the emotionally charged opinions of others. For this reason, emotion is seldom on display or is highly controlled.

In public life, Power People are fairly impervious to the opinions of others, which is why they are often assigned to lead others. The Love Person, however, is seldom given nor wants authority over others. The Love person therefore has difficulty having empathy with the role a Power Person takes on. Most importantly, they do not feel the weight of responsibility.

Power's Frustration with Love

The Love Person wants everyone to have a sense of well-being with no one left behind, but this is not the way life usually functions. Triage nurses in hospitals, for example, must decide which patient needs attention over the next.

The Power Person may not understand the Love Person's empathic concern for all of humanity, seeing it as an unnecessary obstacle to getting things done.

The Power Person may easily find a Love Person to be reactionary, dramatic, and lacking in the ability to plan or delegate when they find themselves overwhelmed.

Power's Contentment with Love

Power People need validation, as does everyone. When Power is put to use in improving well-being, the Power Person enjoys the most rewarding validation through positive feedback from the Love People, over whom they wield the power.

The Love Person provides evidence the Power Person is effective, efficient and a valuable member of the group or society at large.

11. Love and Love Interaction

Regarding relationships and any identical Life Themes: mutual contentment comes with this similarity but any two people are still unique unto themselves even though they share Themes. Conflict can arise.

Love People are always focused on the passionate side of life and they often lack structure.

Love People are naturally drawn to one another in social circles and causes, as they share priorities and sensibilities. However, this pairing is not so common for close personal relationships, presumably because the sameness does not necessarily serve unique individuals. It is more common to see a Love Person paired with a Justice Person.

A Love Person and a Love Person

Love's Frustration with Love

Love People together can produce some challenges if they are too similar. While they share similar strengths there is no one to offset any weakness such as the general lack of structure. They may think all they need is each other but the bill collector will see it differently. The practical and planning aspects of life may fall into disarray when emphasis is placed on feelings "in the now" without regard to planning and consequences. This is why the structured Justice person will make a better life mate.

Love's Contentment with Love

A Love Person in the company of another Love Person usually feels right at home. Mutual appreciation, sharing of life's pleasures and compassion are the reward here, along with abundant emotional support for one another provided they share the same goals.

12. Wisdom and Justice Interaction

The Justice Theme consists of part Love and part Wisdom, so a **Justice Person** finds kinship with either a **Wisdom Person** or a Love Person, depending on which of these is more dominant within the Justice Person. A good example is if the Justice Person expresses 70% Wisdom and 30% Love. The Wisdom person will occasionally find the 30% Love mildly irritating but certainly worth the relationship.

A Wisdom Person and a Justice Person

To the Wisdom Person, compassion for others is based on knowing their full circumstances. Wisdom people tend to feel justified in helping only those who help themselves—those who make an effort to learn more about a situation.

Wisdom's Frustration with Justice: The Wisdom Person may feel frustrated at the Justice Person's endless weighing of options and avoidance of decision-making or action-taking.

Wisdom People get especially frustrated when a Justice Person takes the side of someone who clearly has done wrong and especially if that person should have known better. The Justice person will create excuses citing moral or ethical issues rather than just actual facts.

If the Justice Person consists of more Love than Wisdom, a Wisdom Person would likely find the Justice Person to be far too emotional, clinging to opinions not backed up by logic and reason.

Wisdom's Contentment with Justice: The Wisdom Person appreciates the Justice Person's inquisitive mind and respect for the Wisdom Person's knowledge. The Justice Person may be easy to direct, minimizing the conflict Love may present to the Wisdom person. After all, Justice People usually want to avoid conflict and struggle. They seek harmony. This helps design a harmonious relationship that is pleasant for both.

A Justice Person and a Wisdom Person

For Justice to function properly, it's necessary to gather knowledge that can impact the issue at hand. So wisdom is just one half of the recipe for Justice People to have a sense of completeness. Love is the other half.

Justice's Frustration with Wisdom: The Justice Person's subjective nature (the focus on the rights of an individual) forces them to sympathize with the unfair conditions that a person find themselves in. The Wisdom Person's objective nature (the focus on the bigger picture apart from the subject) directs them to find the logical resolution, independent of or even to the detriment of a single person.

For this reason, a Wisdom Person may ignore the subjective emotional needs of people, which the Justice Person is likely to find unfair or even cruel.

Justice's Contentment with Wisdom: Since the Wisdom Person is driven to know, the Justice Person views the Wisdom Person as an inexhaustible and valuable resource for gathering all the available data that interests the Justice Person.

This allows the Justice person to feel confident he or she possesses all essential facts, which primes them toward effective action. Knowing they can make the "right" decision and avoid the shame or regret of being unjust, the Justice Person finds contentment.

13. Wisdom and Power Interaction

This pairing is extremely common, and usually represents the best match for Power People in close personal relationships. They complement each other very well.

A Wisdom Person and a Power Person

A Wisdom Person prefers power to be implemented only after all available knowledge is accumulated. We have all heard that knowledge is power. A Power person respects those who are knowledgeable as they represent the foundation of a resource of power.

Wisdom's Frustration with Power

Power people are usually very practical in implementing their authority. That is, believing truth is what works best. They want to get to the desired result without waste and generate immediate and efficient results. This explains why, when the Power Person encounters a negative event or result while on their watch, they tend to react quickly. They need resolution to get back on track so as not tarnish the justification for being given the position of authority. They come to a conclusion and quickly implement a remedy. Without further exploring other less practical alternatives, their approach may miss a better long-term goal. Practical thinkers follow a linear directive mode, an innate talent that also enables Power People to lead. Wisdom People always want to know "why" and leave no stone unturned. When Power People believe the end justifies the means and thereby skip fact finding for brevity, they become frustrated.

While the Wisdom Person understands the Power Person is a "change agent", he or she may feel the collateral damage caused by the Power Person's urge to act quickly can outweigh the intended positive result.

Wisdom's Contentment with Power

The Power Person gets things done and is willing to take a stand, accept responsibility (especially where others will not or cannot), and defend their position. This makes them highly reliable and admirable in the eyes of the Wisdom Person. The Power Person is able to put the Wisdom Person's knowledge into practical use. Wisdom People know intuitively not to restrain Power People giving them the freedom to be themselves (powerful).

A Power Person and a Wisdom Person

Power People have a closeness with Wisdom People. After all, knowledge is the main source of their Power to change. Power People seek knowledge if he or she feels it will empower their efforts. But the knowledge they seek must have purpose and be practical, otherwise such knowledge is considered irrelevant.

Another benefit to the Power Person is Wisdom People are not immediately interested in power. They are more than happy to give Power People plenty of space. Wisdom People are driven to deeply know and understand others including those of Power. They understand the needs of Power People and are not intimidated or overwhelmed by them. Rather, they hold a fascination. Wisdom People know Power People are driven by the need to express responsibility, authority, and direction of others. Love, Justice and, occasionally, other Power People, often erroneously see the actions of Power People as trying to personally dominate and take control away from them. Their Life Theme is simply acting out as do all of our Life Themes.

Power's Frustration with Wisdom

The Power Person may feel frustrated with the Wisdom Person's slow pace or reluctance to act. They need to engage in various processes including the mental research for alternatives, which takes time. Walking up to a Wisdom Person and demanding, "just do this," is often met with resistance. Wisdom needs time to ask and understand the various reasons why. A practical Power Person can get very annoyed.

While knowledge is essential to Power, the wrong knowledge can also take power away by making a Power Person wrong

Power's Contentment with Wisdom

Again, what is interesting for the Power Person is that the Wisdom Person has no interest in assuming the power role, even though they have all of the general requirements. That means a Power Person will realize a great deal of support from a Wisdom associate or life mate. However, if demands are made that are very shortsighted, the Wisdom Person will rebel.

With the Wisdom Person's cooperation and support, the Power Person is able to reach and demonstrate high levels of expression.

The Wisdom Person provides knowledge, which is transformed into Power by the Power Person. For this reason, Wisdom People and other Power People are the only ones who the Power Person is willing to listen to. They realize knowledge determines the degree of their success in achievement.

14. Wisdom and Wisdom Interaction

Wisdom People may be drawn to one another in social circles, projects and causes, perhaps because they need to work together in some capacity to synergistically combine their individual knowledge. However, in terms of close personal relationships, a Wisdom Person and another Wisdom Person is a relatively rare combination unless other motivations are sufficiently diverse.

A Wisdom Person and a Wisdom Person

These two may be competitive with one another, causing animosity and power struggles. In a practical sense, the realities of life may be left unattended while learning is favored over doing or balancing things out. If they are able to truly see the value in the other's type and kind of knowledge then cooperation is possible. However, where there are opposing attitudes and perspectives regarding the same facts, fireworks can be expected.

Wisdom's Contentment with Wisdom

A lot of lively conversation is the reward here, as these Wisdom People explore and share in a variety of topics that interest them. Again, when mutual respect is maintained and each Wisdom Person holds a separate "niche" within the relationship, a happy co-existence is possible.

15. Justice and Power Interaction

This combination definitely falls under the category of strange bedfellows. Rare, but still entirely possible with enough awareness and mutual understanding, a relationship between a **Justice Person** and a **Power Person** is far more likely to be fruitful if the Justice Person favors Wisdom over Love in his or her personal mixture of the two virtues.

Justice People may desire power as an ability to influence change. They believe they deserve such power given their moral and ethical insight. Yet, they tend to avoid positions requiring the full force objective power requires in order to avoid potential conflict.

A Justice Person and a Power Person

Like everything else in the Justice Person's world, Power is seen as dualistic. On the one hand, the Justice Person desires power to make things right. On the other hand, the Justice Person is reluctant to seize power, and is suspicious of those who do because they are seen as likely to abuse their power and harm others.

Justice's Frustration with Power: The Justice Person may view the Power Person's behavior and communication as rash, reckless and lacking in fairness or compassion. Power seldom considers the emotional impact of what they do and how others may feel. As long as their criticism is practical and accurate, they feel they have the right to let loose on others, frustrating the Justice People.

Justice's Contentment with Power: Justice finds contentment with Power when the Power Person assumes a leadership role that empowers others or furthers a cause which encompasses human values. They often work well provided they are focused on the same goal. While the Power Person just wants to get the job done, the Justice Person may be looking for perfection.

In an ideal partnership, the Justice Person helps to mold, design, and inform the Power Person's actions. The Power Person inspires the Justice Person to temper his or her perfectionism so results can be enjoyed sooner.

A Power Person and a Justice Person

Fairness seldom comes into play for the Power Person. Rather, the Power Person is directed toward a set goal after emotions and feelings have been considered. The goals have been thoroughly discussed at the executive level and directives have been dispensed. What is seen as unfair would be any event that unnecessarily impedes the intended achievement.

Power's Frustration with Justice: Justice People often fail to take a stand. When they do, they usually need the support of a consensus of opinion or a prescribed course of action.

This foot-dragging frustrates the action-oriented Power Person, who may not understand the Justice Person's need to weigh in factors that seem irrelevant. This dual mode of operation is seen as wasted time.

Power's Contentment with Justice: The Justice Person is likely to give the Power Person all the room he or she needs to work and get the job done. The Justice Person seldom complains and is excellent at carrying out the plans Power may have, especially those involving the need for design and harmonious execution.

If these two can act in concert, they can achieve great things. The Power Person provides the drive and the Justice Person handles the finer details of whatever project they choose to tackle together.

John's Case Study: CLASHING CAREER CHOICES

I met a father and daughter who weren't seeing eye to eye. Their relationship was strained because the father, an attorney, insisted his daughter enroll in college as an International Studies major. The daughter did so, was miserable and started failing. This distressed her father and made him think about making changes in funding her education. Meanwhile, the daughter was feeling called to be a child psychologist, which her father could not understand. As a result, she was scared to talk with him.

During the assessment session, we discovered the father was a Power Person and the daughter, a Justice Person. The daughter wanted to right the wrongs done to children. International business held no lure for her because it lacked the Love component. The father valued international business because of the respect and money he earned which gained him Power.

Both father and daughter learned a great deal about the other during the assessment process. They gained newfound respect and appreciation for each other. The daughter changed her major and began to excel in her studies because they aligned with her Authentic Virtue. The father was filled with appreciation. He stated, "you have shown me a daughter I never knew I had."

John's Case Study: PROMOTION COMMOTION

I did an assessment for a woman who was very skilled, very intelligent and well educated, but she hadn't enjoyed much success in the career realm.

I quickly determined that she was a Justice Person. Understanding the Justice Life Theme, as well as the other Themes, was incredibly eye-opening for her.

It explained why she had had so many run-ins with those in power. In her words: "Now I totally see it. They were Power People and I thought they were being really rude and ruthless... and they kind of are, but now I understand them better. Thank you for bringing me the gift of compassion."

She had bypassed a number of opportunities for advancement because she was reluctant to "seize power" and "dominate" other people. The assessment and explanation of the Justice Theme made her realize this is a built-in tendency for Justice People, and she could choose differently if she wanted to. She felt the information arrived at the perfect time in her life, because she was mature enough to become a good leader. She was inspired by the Power People's ability to get things done, but was determined to do it her way, with Love.

16. Justice and Justice Interaction

Justice People are naturally drawn to one another in social circles, projects and causes, as they share priorities and sensibilities.

They often work together, and it's also a fairly common pairing in close personal relationships. Two Justice people as intimate partners can work if one partner has more Love and the other partner has more Wisdom.

A Justice Person and a Justice Person

Justice's Frustration with Justice

With Justice People there is a lot of perfecting, balancing, and optimizing. If two Justice People have the same ratio of Love to Wisdom, then competition and bickering can occur. Keep in mind, they are still individuals with two different worldviews.

Justice's Contentment with Justice: Two Justice People can understand each other on a deep level. They may not see eye to eye, but they are fundamentally the same in their approach to life.

They can be excellent springboards and supporters for each other's ideas, helping to fine-tune and co-create solutions to various situations. When working together harmoniously, two Justice People can inspire one another to design and enact great things to serve humanity.

17. Power and Power Interaction

The **Power Person** may be attracted to those who are empowered to act and get things done, and often that type of person is another Power Person.

Indeed, Power People are naturally drawn to one another in social circles, projects and causes, as they stand out above the crowd in pushing the action forward.

Either the two Power People will join forces or they will readily compete with each other, and often it is the latter. The Power Person is furiously loyal to those with greater power or when they agree on goals (while considering others as pawns to get the job done). But these roles can shift, and loyalties are likely to shift accordingly.

A Power Person and a Power Person

Power's Frustrations with Power

When Power People clash, it is likely because one person wants Power for the sake of Power and the other person wants to empower for the sake of empowering others.

Power's Contentment with Power: When Power People openly support one another it's extremely gratifying. A respected fellow Power Person can elevate a Power Person's self-esteem as no other Life Theme can.

With a high degree of personal integrity, if two Power People support one another unconditionally, they can achieve great things. Situations will fare better in which two Power People have complimentary careers, rather than directly competing roles.

SECTION IV
PUTTING THE JOHN VORIS METHOD INTO ACTION IN YOUR LIFE

18. Why This is Not Another Personality Profiling Test

Throughout this book, I've demonstrated how the John Voris Method is not a personality-profiling test. This explains how I have been able to help those who did not find satisfaction through common profile tests offered today. Often, one who takes a personality test feels temporarily gratified, but ultimately feels unsatisfied with the information's ability to create lasting and meaningful change in their life. If you are satisfied with any other of those methods, training, learned techniques or tests, know this method was not designed for you.

The Life Themes I've described go beyond the personality. They speak to your unchanging, underlying inner identity. Getting in touch with this Authentic part of yourself is truly life changing.

When you learn (or remember) who you really are, and feel bolstered in simply being you, the positive changes that ensue are unmistakable and unforgettable. When you discover the other people in your life may be fundamentally different from you in that they embody different Life Themes, true healing is the result.

The foundation to the John Voris Method was generated through the application of what is known as Phenomenological Psychology to everyday life experiences. Phenomenological Psychology incorporates the necessary and universal psychological structures that describe the possibility of human experience. These structures are universal to the human species and therefore do not resemble Western Psychology.

The Life Theme is heavily influenced by European psychology rather than the American approach. European psychologists ask the question "What does it mean to be human?" whereas American psychologists focus more on behaviorism which requires observable, repeatable and statistical data that, by definition, eliminates the direct study of the mind.

Most people who have learned and consciously activated their Life Theme say it was a transformative experience.

There are many additional aspects to your Authentic Identity that are beyond the scope of this introductory book. I invite you to please visit www.JohnVoris.com to learn more or to book a private session with me.

19. Why the John Voris Method Works

Now that you've learned about the four Life Themes and about how they interact with one another, you can start putting the John Voris Method into action in your life.

The John Voris Method is based on classical philosophical values that have stood the test of time. These values have been analyzed and utilized in a brand new, radically different, and effective way.

The Life Theme system has been gleaned through real-world observations and correlated with classic philosophy insights. Over and over again, these Life Themes have been organically demonstrated by people from all walks of life. With over twenty years of sustained results now, it is most certainly a natural phenomenon that has been observed or discovered, rather than a neatly invented theory. Much like music or mathematics, we use our minds to notice and make sense of patterns. But as human beings, we did not invent those patterns.

In other words, results came first and the naming and categorizing of Life Themes emerged from actual life experience. What's really fascinating about your Life Theme is that it originates beyond the human personality. It represents what primarily motivates your everyday decisions. There are only four distinctly different Life Themes, but your Authentic Identity applies that theme to make your own personal expression truly unique.

20. How to Use the John Voris Method in Your Life

Each one of us embodies all four of the Life Themes. That is, we all experience Love, Wisdom, Justice, and Power in various forms throughout the day and throughout our lives. And yet, the ways in which we perceive and experience these same four Life Themes can vary radically from one person to the next. Through the Life Theme system, we are able to see clearly and honor our differences, making it possible and even easy for us to have healthier relationships with one another.

Authentically knowing ourselves allows us to make better choices. We can begin to see our own patterns of involvement, of happiness and unhappiness, of satisfaction and dissatisfaction. With a newfound comprehension of the "why" factors, we're empowered to make positive changes.

Your Life Theme—whether it's Love, Wisdom, Justice, or Power—colors, informs and tempers the other three types of experiences for you. It serves as a lens or a filter through which you see the world, and determines how you go about things. It accurately explains what motivates your actions and interactions with others.

Likewise, the other people in your life are working with their own particular Life Themes, and theirs may or may not be the same theme as yours. Understanding other people's Themes helps you to see them for who they truly are. Whether it's your spouse, child, co-worker, neighbor or even a public figure, you will be able to comprehend what motivates them and then choose accordingly how you wish to interact with them.

First and foremost, discovering and understanding your own Life Theme helps you to know yourself more authentically. That leads to letting yourself off the hook more often, growing your self-esteem, and getting clear about the types of work situations and relationships that are, or are not, conducive to your personal happiness.

- Why do you favor certain things and detest others?
- Why do you have a hard time communicating with one person, yet easily get along with another?
- Why do you easily succeed at some endeavors yet struggle in other areas of your life?

Your Life Theme holds the fascinating answers.

Life Themes knowledge has been applied with great success in dating, sales and marketing, counseling, and other arenas. There really is no limit to its usefulness because it speaks to who we truly are. As the ancient Greek philosophers pointed out, to know thyself is a many splendored thing.

In understanding your Life Theme, you're able to quickly enhance and bolster your own unique self-expression, rather than continuing to measure yourself against others who may or may not share your Theme. You will likely experience a noticeable shift away from conformity—and into self-validation. What's more, the personal benefits you reap affect the other people in your life, and even ripple out to benefit all of humanity.

There are always ruts in the road of life, but in knowing your Authentic Identity, you turn on the lights so you can steer around those ruts instead of blindly driving into them.

There is more to your Authentic Identity than your Life Theme, but this book gives you a very useful overview from an excellent starting point.

When the issue involves a family, I like to do assessments for all of the close family members whenever possible. The reason is that relationships are the foundation of life and also the cause of much misunderstanding and stress.

In that spirit, I hope you will share the information contained in this book with others in your life so as many people as possible will experience the gift of self-validation through knowing their Authentic Selves.

SECTION V
ABOUT THE AUTHOR

John W. Voris brings together ancient wisdom, European philosophy and psychology for the purpose of empowering humanity. He earned his Bachelor's Degree in Philosophy from the University of California at Berkeley.

For decades, John Voris has researched European scholars and experts in the fields of Philosophy, Sociology, Forensics, Archeology, Psychology, and other disciplines to uncover what his clients say is missing from American self-help sources. He he broke down the wisdom found in the European sources of Epistemology, Phenomenology, Existentialism and Austrian Praxiology into teachable formulas found in this book. He successfully used his formulas of information for over 20 years to earn a very nice living.

He learned the major reasons why some people succeeded and others failed even though they shared similar education levels and career paths. But with learning techniques in isolating the motivations of others he was also able to apply his discoveries to: career selection, dating, interoffice conflict, isolating individual happiness, how to avoid conflict, effective hiring practices, effective job delegation, even jury selection and much more.

Based on his own real-world observations and supported by his own field experience and the wisdom from hundreds of philosophers and psychologists throughout the centuries, John put together the puzzle pieces and solved many mysteries The Life Themes emerged, describing so well the differences between people that surface factors and facts could not explain.

He discovered the most effective way to communicate is different if you are talking with a Justice Person, a Love Person, a Power Person, or a Wisdom Person. John learned to interpret symbols in the person's environment and other factors that quickly allowed him to speak that person's Life Theme "language." His sales results far exceeded expectations or statistics in his industry.

About Authentic Systems

John Voris retired from sales in early 2000. He wanted to create programs and train people with the methods he'd discovered. He begin by teaching salespeople and executive coaches to use his Life Themes concepts.

Jonathan Rogers joined John in 2007. Jonathan became a student of John's teachings and formalized many of John's concepts into a web-based model to be used for professionals and small businesses.

In 2018, John made the decision to focus entirely on doing personal assessments and bringing his work directly to individuals.

Although he still offers sales training and coaching packages, John has expanded his reach into the mainstream in order to share this valuable information with even more people. John offers individual assessments for those who want more in-depth information about themselves.

There are many additional aspects to your Authentic Identity that are beyond the scope of this introductory book. Please visit www.JohnVoris.com to learn more or to book a private session with John.

John Voris has two daughters who are both artists. He lives in Carmel, California, with his wife Kathleen, a Power Person who founded and operates an elder care home.

Definitions

The Four Universal Virtues

The search for the universal composition of humanity is older than the famous Ancient Greek aphorism inscribed at the Temple of Apollo at Delphi: "know thyself."

Of course, ancient philosophers did not know of psychology in its modern form, nor did they have the skill to explore the human psyche at that point. Their focus was more on the general human condition and the influences of day-to-day human life.

The commonly adopted view at that time was that humans were driven by four spirits. The two most prominent thinkers on the subject were Plato (340 B.C.) and Galen (190 A.D.), a famous physician. Plato asserted the four characteristics to personality were: Artisan (Justice), Guardian (Power), Idealist (Love) and Rational (Wisdom).

Angeles Arrien, Ph.D., was an anthropologist who lectured worldwide. She demonstrated the connection between anthropology, psychology, and religions as they relate to our modern lives in her book "The Four-Fold Way" in 1993. Dr. Arrien explored the nature and fundamental role of each of the four archetypes: the Warrior, the Healer, the Visionary, and the Teacher.

The ultimate purpose of the Warrior, according to Dr. Arrien, is to affect change through power. To affect change, an aspect of the present must die, followed by a rebirth. The Healer, on the other hand, demonstrates empathy and compassion. The Visionary has a dual purpose in being able to see negatives and positives at once, projecting harmony into the future. The Teacher learns of the world and passes this knowledge on to others.

Dr. Arrien's four archetypes are very similar to those of Carl Jung: Rebirth, Mother, Trickster, and Spirit.

Each archetype draws on the deepest mythic roots of humanity, and we too can tap into their timeless wisdom. When we learn to live these archetypes within ourselves, we begin to heal ourselves and our fragmented world.

Almost all of the preceding archetypal systems (plus others not mentioned here) can be correlated to Four Universal Virtues that have been discussed since the beginning of the written word. They are mentioned in the Bible as the attributes of God. The Toltec teachings of Mesoamerica also focus on four universal elements: Love, Wisdom, Justice, and Power.

And so it is with Life Themes: Love, Justice, Wisdom, and Power.

Virtues/Motivation/Purpose

Aristotle, who wrote Nicomachean Ethics, said happiness is the goal of all humanity. It is our qualities which assist in this pursuit and these qualities are called virtues. A virtue is a property of character that allows for and propels success of purpose. It is often said what we value is the target of our actions. Our virtue is a quality used in our actions to capture and retain what we value. Curiosity is a virtue for the Wisdom driven. Caring is a virtue for the Love driven. The desire for symmetry is a virtue for the Justice driven, and the need for Change is a virtue for the Power driven. Therefore, the virtues you hold most valuable reveal your ultimate life purpose.

Explore the description of each word and see which ones best reveal your dominating inner quality. We all express forgiveness, for example, but under what conditions, for what reasons and to what degree? We're all helpful to others at times but why? Under what conditions and why do we help those we do?

Love Life Theme

Appreciate	Freely expressing gratitude.
Caring	Attention to what we value and those around us.
Charity	A giving to those less fortunate
Cheerfulness	Always looking for the good in life while ignoring the bad
Compassion	Deep empathy for the suffering of others
Consideration	Thoughtful care for the needs of others
Faith	Trusting in the sacred to help guide them in life
Forgiveness	Overlooking the mistakes of others even when horrid.
Gentleness	Mental and physical softness lacking willingness to take action
Helpful	Actions that assist others to reach their goal
Selfless	Concern for others to the detriment of self.
Simplicity	Transparency and the lack of complexity
Empathy	Identification with the feelings and motives of others

Wisdom Life Theme

Caution	Avoidance of rash decisions due to thoughtful deliberation
Curiosity	Insatiable desire to know others and the environment
Defiant	Bold resistance supported by unswerving knowledge
Discernment	To distinguish and discriminate the differences of qualities
Discretion	To withhold acquired information from being misunderstood
Endurance	Perseverance and patience in the face of obstacles.
Fidelity	Acknowledgement of agreements
Determination	Firmness of purposeful meaning as motivation
Devotion	Loyalty driven by caring in the form of respect
Diligence	Giving effective attention to a task.
Magnanimity	To engage into actions for noble purposes
Patience	The ability to endure pain and hardship
Tact	Getting results despite possibly offending others
Understanding	Comprehension of facts and the rationale of others
Idealism	Elevated ideas pursuing ideals over physical motivations

Justice Life Theme

Acceptance	Bending with the obstacles of life and not breaking
Beauty	Reverence for harmony and a sense of wonder
Balance	To give equal attention and consideration to all things
Cooperation	Working with others toward a common goal
Creativity	The ability to reify alternate realities.
Contentment	The awareness and acceptance of sufficiency
Devotion	Commitment to what we care about with zeal.
Dignity	Honoring the worth of all people with respect
Diligence	Concentration and focused attention
Fairness	Ensuring everyone's needs are met without harming others
Friendliness	Reaching out to others and willingness to be vulnerable
Honesty	Revealing truth regardless of the negative impact on self
Righteousness	To live by an inner code of conduct we know is right
Honor	Living with self-respect following our virtuous character
Thrift	Avoiding the unnecessary and focusing on utility
Symmetry	The equal proportion of parts of a whole in form

Power Life Theme

Accountable	The demand to assume responsibility for your decisions
Assertiveness	Bold, confident proclamations and declarations
Aggressive	Vigorously energetic initiatives and forcefulness
Bravery	To face danger or unpleasantness without displaying fear
Commitments	To carry out with purpose
Confidence	To feel personal power and faith in ones abilities
Decisiveness	Firmness of mind in taking a stand displaying courage
Detachment	To feel emotions without allowing them to control us
Determination	Firmness of purpose
Responsible	To be accountable for events associated with our choices
Excellence	To generate results above expectations
Fortitude	Strength of mind to endure adversity with courage
Loyalty	Allegiance to others of power
Impatience	Eagerness for change

The Power of Four

The reason for this list is to first demonstrate how often our findings from exploring the human species have been broken down into a grouping of four. This includes four aspects. types, kinds, elements, philosophical components, functions, and descriptions. Given that many of these findings can be traced to the beginning of history, they may not reflect findings in reality but how the mind and brain interpret the world. This includes describing the round earth in four cardinal directions of North, South, East, and West. This may cause a person to ask, how can the round earth have four corners?

Science
Four Basic States of Matter

1. Solid
2. Liquid
3. Gas
4. Plasma

Four-Dimensional Space

1. Height
2. Width
3. Depth
4. Time

The Four Canons of Science

These are the four fundamental principles that appear to be accepted by almost all scientists.

1. Determinism
2. Empiricism
3. Parsimony
4. Testability

Physical Human Body
Four Base Elements:

1. Hydrogen
2. Oxygen
3. Nitrogen
4. Carbon

Body Tissue Types:

1. Connective
2. Epithelial
3. Muscular
4. Nervous

Blood Types (Phenotypes):

1. A
2. B
3. AB
4. O

DNA: Four Nucleic Acids: ACGT

1. Adenine
2. Cytosine
3. Guanine
4. Thymine

Brain Chemical Systems: Personality Traits

1. Dopamine/Nor-epinephrine
2. Serotonin
3. Testosterone
4. Estrogen/Oxytocin

Philosophy
Four Causes – Aristotelian Science

1. Formal cause – (of Being)
2. Material cause – (of Knowledge)
3. Efficient cause – (of Becoming)
4. Final cause – (of Action)

Four Forms of Experience

The "I" is the Synthetic motivation generated from our external physical changing environment through dialogue.

The "Am" is the Authentic motivation generated from our internal abstract stable sense of self.

- 1 The Inner Experience of I (I am) is Experience.
- 2 The Outer Appearance of I (I am) is Behavior.

- 3 The Inner Experience of World is Communication.
- 4 The Outer Appearance of World is Science.

Table of Judgments by Immanuel Kant

1. Quantity
2. Quality
3. Relation
4. Modality

Four Methods of Firm Beliefs by C. S. Peirce

1. Tenacity
2. Authority
3. A Priori
4. Scientific

Four Barriers to Inquiry by C. S. Peirce

1. Assertion of absolute certainty – Power
2. Maintaining that something is absolutely unknowable – Wisdom
3. Maintaining that something is absolutely inexplicable – Love
4. Holding that perfect exactitude is possible – Justice

Education
Four Stage Decision Cycle by John Boyd

1. Observation (data intake through the senses)

2. Orientation (analysis and synthesis of data)
3. Decision (Choice)
4. Action (Power)

Four Modes of Inquiry by Richard McKeon

1. of Being (Being)
2. of Thought (That which is)
3. of Fact (Existence)
4. of Simplicity (Experience)

Four Category Ontology by Jonathan Lowe (E.J. Lowe)

1. Kinds (substantial universals)
2. Attributes (relational universals and property-universals)
3. Objects (substantial particulars)
4. Modes (relational particulars and property-particulars)

<u>Mind Identity</u>
Four Universal Virtues or Life Themes:

1. Love
2. Justice
3. Wisdom
4. Power

Four Worlds of Possibilities (Amit Go swami – Quantum Activist)

1. Material Possibilities – Physical (Synthetic)

2. Vital Possibilities – Feel (Authentic)
3. Mental Possibilities – Think (Synthetic)
4. Supramental Possibilities – Intuit (Authentic)

Four Worldviews (Function) by Stephen C. Peper

1. Formism (Analytic, Dispersive) – Realism – **Justice**
2. Mechanism (Analytic, Integrative) – Materialism – **Wisdom**
3. Contextualism (Synthetic, Dispersive) – Pragmatism – **Power**
4. Organicism (Synthetic, Integrative) – Idealism – **Love**

Four World-Views by Erich Adickes

1. Dogmatic (or Doctrinaire) – **Power**
2. Agnostic (or Skeptical) – **Justice**
3. Traditional – **Love**
4. Innovative – **Wisdom**

Four Mistaken Goals by Alfred Adler

1. Recognition – **Wisdom**
2. Power – **Power**
3. Service – **Love**
4. Revenge – **Justice**

Four Dimensions of Temperament by Arnold Buss and Robert Plomin

1. Emotionality-Impassiveness

2. Sociability-Detachment
3. Activity-Lethargy
4. Impulsivity-Deliberateness

Four Abnormal Behaviors of Temperament by Ernst Kretschmer

1. Hyperesthetic
2. Anesthetic
3. Melancholic
4. Hypomanic

Four Aspects of Discipline by M. Scott Peck

1. Delaying gratification
2. Acceptance of responsibility
3. Dedication to truth
4. Balancing

Four Stages of Human Spiritual Development by M. Scott Peck

1. Stage 1: Egoistic and lacking empathy
2. Stage 2: Blind faith in authority and a willingness to obey
3. Stage 3: Scientific skepticism and questioning
4. Stage 4: Mystical loving others as yourself, loss of ego, genuine forgiveness

Four Worldview Questions by Brian J. Walsh and J. Richard Middleton

1. Who am I? – what is the nature, task and significance of human beings?
2. Where am I? – what is the origin and nature of the reality in which human beings find themselves?
3. What's wrong? – how can we account for the distortion and brokenness in this reality?
4. What's the remedy? – how can we alleviate this brokenness, if at all?

The Four Noble Truths of Buddhism (Negative/Suffering):

1. Dukkha – Life means suffering.
2. Samudaya – The origin of suffering is attachment.
3. Nirodha – The cessation of suffering is attainable.
4. Magga – The path to the cessation of suffering.

Four Saṃhitās (Vedic Ancient Hindu)
Vedic texts or śruti collections of metrical material known as of which the first three are related to the performance of yajna (sacrifice) in historical Vedic religion:

1. **The Rigveda**, containing hymns to be recited by the hotar, or presiding priest;
2. **The Yajurveda**, containing formulas to be recited by the adhvaryu or officiating priest;
3. **The Samaveda**, containing formulas to be sung by the udgatar or priest that chants;
4. **The Atharvaveda**, a collection of spells and incantations,

apotropaic charms and speculative hymns.

Four Things Support the World by Muhammad

1. The learning of the wise,
2. The justice of the great,
3. The prayers of the good
4. The valor of the brave

Biblical Symbolic Meaning of the Number 4

1. Universality
2. Symmetry
3. Equal
4. Balance

Four Rivers in the Garden of Eden

1. Pishon (Jaxartes or Syr Darya)
2. Gihon (Oxus or Amu Darya)
3. Hiddekel (Tigris)
4. P'rat (Euphrates)

Four Standards/Banners/Emblems of ancient Jewish tribes

1. Creature: Lion
2. Color: Green
3. Tribe: Judah
4. Position: East

Miscellaneous
Four Stages of the Creative Process

1. Preparation (of Being)
2. Incubation (of Knowledge)
3. Illumination (of Becoming)
4. Verification (of Action)

Four Primal Human Forces of Will by Neil Kramer

1. Creation
2. Destruction
3. Solidity
4. Yielding

Arithmetic Four Basic Mathematical Operations or The Basis of Calculations

1. Add – Animus
2. Subtract – Anima
3. Multiply – Animus
4. Divide – Anima

Primary Colors RGBY:

1. Red
2. Green
3. Blue
4. Yellow (Gold)

Precious Stones:

All other stones are semi-precious

1. Ruby (Red) Assertive
2. Emerald (Green) Slow Process
3. Sapphire (Blue) Passive
4. Diamond (Yellow) Assertive

Classical Greek Elements

1. Fire
2. Earth
3. Water
4. Wind

Seasons:

1. Spring
2. Summer
3. Fall
4. Winter

Directions:

1. North
2. South
3. East
4. West

Friedrich Nietzsche – The Will to Power

1. Will to power as Art (Human Symbolic Affirmation)

2. Will to power as Knowledge (Linguistic Descriptions)
3. Will to power as Society (Social Conventions)
4. Will to power as Nature (Abstract or Physical Production)

Apollo at Delphi

1. Know thyself – Wisdom
2. Choose Yourself – Justice
3. Accept your Destiny – Love
4. Become who you are – Power

Four Forms of Taxation

1. Income
2. Corporate
3. Property
4. Sales

Bibliography

Abel, Reuben. Man is the Measure. New York: The Free P, 1976.

Adorno, Theodor W. The Culture Industry. London: Routledge, 1991.

Aitchison, Jean. The Language Web. New York: Cambridge UP, 1997.

Allport, Gordon W. The Nature of Prejudice. Garden City, NY: Doubleday Anchor Books, 1958.

Althusser, Louis. On Ideology. London: Verso, 2008

Ambrose, Alice, ed. Wittgenstein's Lectures. Amherst, New York: Prometheus Books, 2001.

Anscombe, G.E.M. Ludwig Wittgenstein: Zettel. Ed. G H. Wright. Berkeley: University of California P, 1967.

Anscombe, G.E.M. Ludwig Wittgenstein on Certainty. Ed. G H. Von Wright. New York: Harper Tourchbooks, 1969.

Ansombe, G.E.M., and G. H. Von Wright, eds. Remarks on the Philosophy of

Arrington, Robert L., and Hans-Johann Glock, eds. Wittgenstein & Quine. London and: Panjandrum Books, Inc., 1982.

Audi, Robert. Epistemology. New York: Routledge, 1998.

Austin, J. L. How to Do Things with Words. Cambridge: Harvard UP, 1975.

Ayer, Alfred J. Language Truth and Logic. New York: Dover Publications, Inc., 1952.

Bachelard, Gaston. The Poetics of Reverie. Trans. Daniel Russell. Boston: Beacon P,

Bayley, Harold. The Lost Language of Symbolism. Escondido, Ca: The Book Tree, 2000.

Becker, Ernest. The Denial of Death. New York: Simon & Schuster, 1997.

Bellatly, Angus, and Oscar Zarate. Introducing Mind & Brain. Lanham: Totem, 1999.

Bennet, Jonathan. Rationality. New York: Routledge & Kegan Paul, 1967.

Berger, John. Ways of Seeing. London 1977: British Broadcasting Corporation.

Berger, Peter L., and Thomas Luckmann. The Social Construction of Reality. New York: Anchor Books, 1967.

Blumer, Herbert. Symbolic Interactionism. Berkeley: University of California P, 1986.

Bolen, Jean S. The Tao of Psychology. Cambridge: Harper & Row, 1979.

Boon, James A. From Symbolism to Structuralism. New York: Harper Tourchbooks, 1972.

Boorstin, Daniel J. The Discoverers. New York: Vintage Books, 1985.

Borst, C.v., comp. The Mind/Brain Identity Theory. New York: St. Martin P, 1973.

Bourdieu, Pierre. Language and Symbolic Power. Cambridge, MA: Harvard UP, 2001.

Bradford, Richard. Roman Jakobson: Life, Language, Art. London: Routledge, 1994.

Bronowski, Jacob. The Origins of Knowledge and Imagination. New Haven: Yale UP, 1978.

Broomfield, John. Other Ways of Knowing. Rochester, Vermont: Inner Traditions, 1997.

Buckland, Raymond. Signs, Symbols, and Omens. St. Paul, MN: Llewellyn Publications, 2003.

Butler, Judith. The Psychic Life of Power. Stanford, CA: Stanford UP, 1997.

Buzan, Tony. Use Both Sides of Your Brain. New York: E.P. Dutton, Inc., 1983.

Bynum, Caroline W. Metamorphosis and Identity. New York: Zone Books, 2005.

Capaldi, Nicholas. The Art of Deception. Amherst, NY: Prometheus Books, 1987.

Capra, Fritjof. The Tao of Physics. Boston: Shambhala, 2000.

Carroll, Noel. The Philosophy of Horror. New York: Routledge.

Cassirer, Ernst. Language and Myth. New York: Dover Publications Inc., 1946.

Cavell, Stanley. The Claim of Reason. New York: Oxford UP, 1999.

Chappell, V. C., ed. The Philosophy of Mind. Englewood Cliffs, NJ: Prentice-Hall, Inc., 1962.

Chisholm, Roderick M. Theory of Knowledge. Englewood Cliffs, NJ: Prentice-Hall, Inc., 1966.

Chodorow, Joan, ed. Encountering Jung on Active Imagination. Princeton: Princeton UP, 1997.

Chomsky, Noam. Language and Thought. Wakefield, RI: Moyer Bell, 2004.

Chomsky, Noam. New Horizons in the Study of Language and Mind. Cambridge: Cambridge UP, 2004.

Chomsky, Noam. On Language. New York: The New P, 1998.

Chomsky, Noam. On Nature and Language. Cambridge: Cambridge UP, 2002.

Cirlot, J. E. A Dictionary of Symbols. Mineola, NY: Dover Publications, Inc., 2002.

Clarke, Robert B. An Order Outside Time. Charlottesville, VA: Hampton Roads Co., Inc., 2005.

Cobley, Paul, and Litza Jansz. Introducing Semiotics. Lanham, Md: Totem Books, 1998.

Cogswell, David. Chomsky for Beginners. London: Writers and Readers Ltd., 1996.

Cohen, Jeffrey J., ed. Monster Theory. Minnesota: University of Minnesota P, 1996.

Cohen, Ted. Jokes: Philosophical Thoughts on Joking Matters. Chicago: The University of Chicago P, 1999.

Collins, Jeff, and Howard Selina. Introducing Heidegger. Lanham, Md: Totem Books, 1999.

Conradi, Peter, ed. Existentialists and Mystics. New York: Penguin Books, 1997.

Cooper, Thomas W. A Time Before Deception. Santa Fe, NM: Clear Light, 1998.

Coplestion, Frederick. A History of Philosophy. Vol. IV. New York: Image Books, 1994.

Cosman, Carol, trans. Wittgenstein Reads Freud: the Myth of the Unconscious. Princeton: New French Thought, 1995.

Cotkin, George. Existential America. Baltimore: The Johns Hopkins UP, 2003.

Crouch, James E. Functional Human Anatomy. Philadelphia: Lea & Febiger, 1970.

Danto, Arthur, and Sidney Morgenbesser. Philosophy of Science. New York: Meridian Books, Inc., 1960.

Darwin, Charles. The Origin of Species. New York: The Modern Library, 1998.

David, Catherine. The Beauty of Gesture. Berkeley, California: North Atlantic Books, 1996.

Davis, Philip E. Moral Duty and Legal Responsibility. New York: Appletion-Century-Crofts Educational Division, 1966.

De Laszlo, Violet S., ed. The Basic Writings of C.G. Jung. Trans. R.f C. Hull. Princeton: Princeton UP, 1990.

Delunas, Eve. Survival Games, Personalities Play. Carmel, Ca: Sunflower Ink, 1992.

Devitt, Michale, and Richard Hanley, eds. Philosophy of Language. Malden: Blackwell, 2006.

Dewey, John. Art as Experience. New York: The Berkley Group, 1980.

Dewey, John. How We Think. Amherst, Ny: Prometheus Books, 1991.

Diamond, Cora, ed. Wittgenstein's Lectures on the Foundation of Mathematics Cambridge, 1939: The University of Chicago, 1975.

Diamond, Jared. Guns, Germs, and Steel. New York: W.W. Norton & Company, 1999.

Dorfman, Ariel. The Empire's Old Clothes. New York: Pantheon Books, 1983.

Dreyfus, Hubert L. Being-in-the-World. Cambridge, MA: The MIT P, 1991.

Dundas, Evalyn T. Symbols Come Alive in the Sand. Boston: Coventure, 1990.

Duranti, Alessandro, ed. Key Terms in Language and Culture. Malden: Blackwell, 2001.

Durkheim, Emile, and Marcel Mauss. Primitive Classification. Trans. Rodney Needham. 1963: University of Chicago P.

Edgar, Andrew, and Peter Sedgwick, eds. Cultural Theory.

London: Routledge, 2002.

Ellul, Jacques. Propaganda. Trans. Konrad Kellen and Jean Lerner. New York: Vintage Books, 1968.

Epstein, Joseph. Snobbery: the American Version. Boston: Houghton Mifflin Company, 2002.

Erickson, Erick H. Identity and the Life Cycle. New York: W.W. Norton & Co., 1994.

Faludi, Susan. Backlash. New York: Anchor Books, 1991. Feifel, Herman, ed. The Meaning of Death. New York: McGraw-Hill Book Company, 1965.

Fernandez, James W., ed. Beyond Metaphor. Stanford, Ca: Stanford UP, 1991.

Field, Joanna. On Not Being Able to Paint. Los Angeles: Jeremy P. Tarcher, Inc., 1976.

Finch, Henry L. The Vision of Wittgenstein. London: Vega, 2001.

Fiske, John. Understanding Popular Culture. London: Routledge, 1989.

Florman, Samuel C. The Existential Pleasures of Engineering. 2nd ed. New York: St. Martin Griffin, 1994.

Fogelin, Robert. Walking the Tightrope of Reason. New York: Oxford UP, 2003.

Fogiel, M. REA's Problem Solvers Psychology. New York: Research and Education Association, 1987.

Forster, Michael N. Wittgenstein on the Arbitrariness of Grammar. Princeton: Princeton UP, 2004.

Forty, Sandra. Symbols. San Diego, Ca: Thunder Bay, 2003. Frank, Francine, and Frank Anshen. Language and the Sexes. Albany: State University of New York P, 1983.

Frankl, Viktor E. Man's Search for Meaning. New York: Washington Square P, 1984.

Frankl, Viktor E. Man's Search for Ultimate Meaning.Cambridge: Perseus, 2000.

Frankl, Viktor E. Recollections. Trans. Joseph Fabry and Judith Fabry. Cambridge: Perseus, 2000.

Frankl, Viktor E. The Doctor and the Soul. Trans. Richard Winston and Clara Winston. New York: Vintage Books, 1986.

Frankl, Viktor E. The Unconscious God. New York: Simon and Schuster, 1975.

Frankl, Viktor E. The Will to Meaning. New York: Penguin Books, 1988.

Frazer, Sir James G. The Golden Bough. Simon & Schuster, 1996.

Freud, Sigmund. The Ego and the Id. New York: W.W. Norton & Co, 1960.

Fussell, Paul. Class. New York: Touchstone Books, 1992.

Gadamer, Hans-Georg. Philosophical Hermeneutics. Trans. David E. Linge. Ed. Berkeley: University of California P, 2004.

Gadamer, Hans-Georg. Truth and Method. 2nd ed. London: Continuum, 2004.

Gardner, Howard. Changing Minds. Boston: Harvard Business School P, 2004.

Gee, James P. An Introduction to Discourse Analysis. London: Routledge, 2003.

Geertz, Clifford. Local Knowledge. 3rd ed. Basic Books, 1983. Geertz, Clifford. The Interpretation of Cultured. New York: Basic Books, 2000.

Gellatly, Angus, and Oscar Zarate. Introducing Mind & Brain. Lanham: Totem Books, 1999.

Gellner, Ernest. Language and Solitude. Cambridge, UK: Cambridge UP, 1998.

Gendler, J. Ruth. The Book of Qualities. New York: Harper Perennial, 1988.

Goff, Oliver Kenneth. Brain-Washing: A *Synthesis of the Russian Textbook on Psychopolitics*. Englewood, CO 1939.

Goffman, Erving. Interaction Ritual. New York: Pantheon Books, 1982.

Gordon, David. Therapeutic Metaphors. Cupertino, Ca: META Publications, 1978.

Goswami, Amit. The Self-Aware Universe. New York: Jeremy P. Tarcher, 1995.

Goswami, Amit. The Visionary Window. Wheaton, Illinois: Quest Books, 2000.

Grayling, A. C. Wittgenstein a Very Short Introduction. Oxford: Oxford UP, 1996.

Grene, Marjorie. Introduction to Existentialism. Chicago: Phoenix Books, 1958.

Grudin, Robert. Time and the Art of Living. New York: Ticknor & Fields, 1982.

Gumbrell, Colin. Karl Marx. London: Evergreen Lives, 1983. Gutting, Gary. French Philosophy in the Twentieth Century. Cambridge: Cambridge UP, 2001.

Hacking, Ian. An Introduction to Probability and Inductive Logic. Cambridge: Cambridge UP, 2001.

Harrison, Lawrence E., and Samuel P. Huntington, eds. Culture Matters. New York: Basic Books, 2000.

Hartmann, Ernest. Boundaries in the Mind. Basic Books, 1991.

Hayakawa, S. I., and Alan R. Hayakawa. Language in Thought and Action. San Diego1990: Harcourt Brace Jovanovich.

Haybron, Daniel M. The Pursuit of Unhappiness. Oxford, 2008

Hegel, G.w. F. Phenomenology of Spirit. Oxford: Oxford UP, 1977.

Hegel, G.w. F. Reason in History. Upper Saddle River, New Jersey: Prentice-Hall, Inc., 1997.

Heidegger, Martin. Discourse on Thinking. Trans. John M. Anderson. New York: Harper Tourchbooks, 1969.

Heidegger, Martin. Existence and Being. Chicago: Henry Regnery Company, 1970.

Heidegger, Martin. Introduction to Metaphysics. Trans. Gregory Fried and Richard Polt. New Haven: Yale UP, 2000.

Heidegger, Martin. On Time and Being. Trans. Joan Stambaugh. Chicago: University of Chicago P, 2002.

Heidegger, Martin. Poetry, Language, Thought. Trans. Albert Hofstadter. New York: Perennial Classics, 2001.

Heidegger, Martin. The Essence of Human Freedom. Trans. Ted Sadler. London: Continuum, 2005.

Heidegger, Martin. What is Called Thinking? Trans. J. Glenn Gray. New York: Perennial, 2004.

Heilbroner, Robert L. The Worldly Philosophers. 3rd ed. New York: Simon and Schuster, 1967.

Heneri, Robert. The Art Spirit. New York: Harper & Row,, 1984.

Herriot, Peter. An Introduction to the Psychology of Language. London: Methuen & Co. Ltd., 1970.

Hintikka, Jaakko. On Wittgenstein. Australia: Wadsworth, 2000.

Hoeller, Stephan A. The Gnostic Jung. Wheaton, IL: Quest Books, 2002.

Hoffer, Eric. The True Believer. New York: Perennial Classics, 2002.

Hofstadter, Douglas R. Metamagical Themas: Questing for the Essence of Mind and Pattern. New York: Basic Books, 1985.

Hopcke, Robert H. Persona. Boston: Shambhala, 1995.

Horkheimer, Max. Eclipse of Reason. London: Continuum, 2004.

Hull, C G. Synchronicity. Trans. R.f. C. Hull. Princeton: Princeton UP, 1973.

Hunt, Morton. The Story of Psychology. New York: Doubleday, 1993.

Husserl, Edmund. Phenomenology. Ed. Joseph J. Kockelmans. Garden City, NY: Anchor Books, 1967.

Hyde, Maggie, and Michael McGuinness. Introducing Jung. Lanham, NJ: Totem Books, 2003.

Innes, Brian. Profile of a Criminal Mind. Pleasantville, NY: The Reader's Digest Association, Inc., 2003.

James, William. A Pluralistic Universe. Lincoln: University of Nebraska P, 1996.

James, William. The Will to Believe. New York: Dover Publications, Inc., 1956.

Jaspers, Karl. Philosophy. Vol. 1. Chicago: University of Chicago P, 1956.

Jaspers, Karl. Reason and Existenz. New N=York: The Noonday P, 1955.

Jaspers, Karl. Way to Wisdom. New Haven: Yale UP, 1962.

Jensen, Derrick. The Culture of Make Believe. White River Junction: Chelsea Green Company, 2004.

Johannesen, Richard L. Ethics in Human Communication. Columbus, OH: Charles E. Merrill Co., 1975.

Johnson, Mark. The Body in the Mind. Chicago: The University of Chicago P, 1987.

Johnston, Derek J. A Brief History of Philosophy Form Socrates to Derrida. London: Continuum, 2006.

Johnston, R. Neville. The Language Codes. Boston: Weiser Books, 2000.

Jourard, Sidney M. The Transparent Self. New York: Van Nostrand Reinhold Co., 1971.

Jung, Carl G. Four Archetypes. Trans. R.f. C. Hull. Princeton: Princeton UP, 1992.

Jung, Carl G. Man and His Symbols. London, Dell. 1964

Jung, Carl G. Two Essays on Analytical Psychology. Trans. R.f. C. Hull. 2nd ed. Princeton: Princeton UP, 1970.

Jung, Carl G. Aspects of the Masculine. Trans. R.f. C. Hull. Princeton: Princeton UP, 1989.

Jung, Carl Modern Man in Search of a Soul. Trans. W. S. Dell and Cary F. Baynes. San Diego: Harcourt, Inc., 1933.

Jung, Carl G. On the Naute of the Psyche. Trans. R.f C. Hull. Princeton: Princeton UP, 1973.

Jung, Carl G. Psychology and the Occult. Trans. R.f. C. Hull. Princeton: Princeton UP, 1981.

Jung, Carl G. The Archetypes and the Collective Unconscious. Trans. R.f. C. Hull. 2ne ed. Princcton: Princeton UP, 1968.

Jung, Carl G. The Spirit in Man, Art and Literature. Trans. R.f. C. Hull. Princeton: Princeton UP, 1978.

Jung, Carl G. The Undiscovered Self. Trans. R.f. C. Hull. Princeton: Princeton UP, 1990.

Kaku, Michio. Parallel Worlds. New York: Doubleday, 2004.

Kandinsky, Wassily. Concerning The Spiritual in Art. New York: Dover Publications, 1977.

Kaufmann, Walter. Critique of Religion and Philosophy. New York: Harper Tourchbooks, 1972.

Kegan, Robert. The Evolving Self. Cambridge, MA: Harvard UP, 2001.

Keller, Helen. The Story of My Life. Ed. James Berger. New York: The Modern Library, 2003.

Keller, Helen. The Story of My Life. Ed. James Berger. New York: The Modern Library, 2004.

Kennedy-Moore, Eileen, and Jeanne C. Watson. Expressing Emotion. New York: The Guilford P, 1999.

Kenny, Anthony, ed. The Wittgenstein Reader. Oxford: Blackwell, 1998.

Kenny, Anthony, trans. Philosophical Grammar. Berkeley: University of California P, 1978.

Kenny, Anthony. Wittgenstein. Cambridge: Harvard UP, 1973.

Kim, Jaegwon. Philosophy of Mind. Boulder, CO: Westview P, 1996.

Koller, John M. Oriental Philosophies. New York: Charles Scribner Sons, 1970.

Korem, Dan. The Art of Profiling. Richardson, Tx: International Focus P, 2003.

Kristeva, Julia. Desire in Language. New York: Columbia UP, 1982.

Kristeva, Julia. Powers of Horror. New York: Columbia UP, 1982.

Lacey, A. R. Modern Philosophy. Boston: Routledge & Kegan Paul, 1982.

Laing, R.d. The Divided Self. London: Penguin Books, 1990.

Lakatos, Imre, and Alan Musgrave, eds. Criticism and the Growth of Knowledge. New York: Cambridge UP, 1970.

Lakoff, George, and Mark Johnson. Metaphors We Live By. Chicago: The University of Chicago P, 1980.

Lawley, James, and Penny Tomkins. Metaphors in Mind. London: The Developing Company P, 2000.

Le Bon, Gustave. The Crowd. New Brunswick: Transaction, 1999.

Lee, David. Cognitive Linguistics, an Introduction. Oxford: Oxford UP, 2003.

Leupin, Alexandre. Lacan Today. New York: Other P, 2004.

Levi-Strauss, Claude. Myth and Meaning. New York: Schocken Books, 1995.

Levi-Strauss, Claude. Structural Anthropology. Basic Books, 1963.

Levi-Strauss, Claude. The View From Afar. Chicago: The University of Chicago P, 1985.

Levinas, Emmanuel. The Theory of Intuition in Husserl's Phenomenology. 2nd ed. Evanston, Illinois: Northwestern UP, 1998.

Levin, David M. The Listening Self. London: Routledge, 1989.

Lewis, M M. Language in Society. London: Thomas Nelson and Sons Ltd., 1947.

Lewontin, R. C. Biology as Ideology. New York: HarperPerennial, 1993.

Lieberman, David J. Instant Analysis. New York: St. Martin Griffin, 1997.

Lippmann, Walter. Public Opinion. New York: The Macmillan Company, 1930.

Lodge, David. Language of Fiction. London: Routledge, 2001.

Lowie, Robert H. Primitive Society. New York: Boni and Liveright, 1920.

Lurie, Alison. The Language of Clothes. New York: Vintage Books, 1981.

Macdonald, Paul S., ed. The Existentialist Reader. New York: Routledge, 2001.

Macey, David. Dictionary of Critical Theory. London: Penguin Books, 2002.

Machiavelli, Niccolo. The Art of War. Da Capo P, 1965.

Machiavelli, Niccolo. The Prince. New York: The New American Library, 1952.

Magee, Bryan. The Philosophy of Schopenhauer. Oxford: Clarendon P, 1997.

Manguel, Alberto. Reading Pictures What We Think About When We Look At Art. New York: Random House, 2002.

Margolis, Michael, and Gary A. Mauser. Manipulating Public Opinion. Pacific Grove, CA: Brooks/Cole Co, 1989.

Marinoff, Lou. Therapy of the Sane. New York: Bloomsbury, 2003.

Masterson, James F. The Search For the Real Self. London: Collier Macmillan, 1988.

Matson, Wallace I. A History of Philosophy. New York: Van Nostrand Reinhold Company, 1968.

Matthews, Caitlin, and John Matthews. Walkers Between the Worlds. Rochester, Vermont: Inner Traditions, 2004.

Matthews, Eric. Merleau-Pontya: Guide for the Perplexed. London: Continuum, 2006.

Matthews, Eric. Twentieth Century French Philosophy. Oxford: Oxford UP, 1996.

May, Rollo, and Ernest Angel eds. Existence a New Dimension in Psychiatry and Psychology. New York: Basic Books,1958.

May, Rollo. Man's Search for Himself. New York: Delta, 1973.

McEvilley, Thomas. Art & Otherness. Kingston, New York: McPherson & Company, 1992.

McFadyen, Ian. Mind Wars. St. Leonard's, Australia: Allen & Unwin, 2000.

McGinn, Colin. The Mysterious Flame. New York: Basic Books, 1999.

McKenna, Terence, and Dennis McKenna. The Invisible Landscape. San Francisco: Harper San Francisco, 1993.

Mead, George H. Mind, Self, and Society. Ed. Charles W. Morris. Chicago: The University of Chicago P, 1967.

Medina, Jose. Language: Key Concepts in Philosophy. London: Continuum, 2005.

Medina, Jose. The Unity of Wittgenstein's Philosophy. Albany: State University of New York P, 2002.

Mehrabian, Albert. Silent Messages. Belmont, Ca: Wadsworth Company, 1981.

Merleau-Ponty, Maurice. Phenomenology of Perception. Trans. Colin Smith. London: Routledged, 2002.

Midgley, David, ed. The Essential Mary Midgley. London: Routledge, 2005.

Miles, T. R. Eliminating the Unconscious. Oxford: Pergamon P, 1966.

Miller, John, and Genevieve Anderson, eds. On Suicide. San Francisco: Chronicle Books, 1992.

Miller, John, comp. Beauty. San Francisco: Chronicle Books, 1997.

Miller, William I. The Anatomy of Disgust. Cambridge, MA: Harvard UP, 1997.

Mills, C. Wright. The Sociological Imagination. Oxford: Oxford UP, 2000.

Moran, Dermot. Introduction to Phenomenology. London: Routledge, 2000.

Murchie, Guy. The Seven Mysteries of Life. Boston: Houghton Mifflin Company, 1999.

Napoli, Donna J. Language Matters. Oxford: Oxford UP, 2003.

Nealon, Jeffrey, and Susan Searls Giroux. The Theory Toolbox. Lanham: Rowman & Littlefield, Inc., 2003.

Nesbitt Shanor, Karen. The Emerging Mind. Los Angeles: Renaissance Books, 1999.

Nichols, Shaun, and Stephen P. Stich. Mindreading. Oxford: Clarendon P, 2003.

Nijinsky, Romola, ed. The Diary of Vaslav Nijinsky. Berkeley: University of California P, 1984.

Olsen, Tillie. Silences. New York: Dell Co, 1983.

Ozick, Cynthia. Metaphor and Memory. New York: Vintage Books, 1989.

Pasternak, Charles. The Essence of Humanity. Chichester: Wileys, 2003.

Peat, F. David. Synchronicity. New York: Bantam Books, 1987.

Perloff, Marjorie. Wittgenstein's Ladder. Chicago: The University of Chicago P, 1996.

Phillips, William, ed. Art and Psychoanalysis. Cleveland: Meridian Books, 1963.

Piaget, Jean. The Child's Conception of the World. Trans. Joan Tomlinson. Lanham: Littlefield Adams Quality Paperbacks.

Piers, Gerhart, and Milton B. Singer. Shame and Guilt. Springfield, IL: Charles C. Thomas, 1953.

Pinker, Steven. The Language Instinct. New York: Perennial Classics, 2000.

Pinker, Steven. The Blank Slate: The Modern Denial of Human Nature. London: Penguin Books, 2002.

Pojman, Louis P. Philosophy the Quest for Truth. 5th ed. Oxford: Oxford UP, 2002.

Polster, Erving & Miriam. Gestalt Therapy Integrated. New York: Vintage Books, 1974.

Popper, Karl R. The Logic of Scientific Discovery. New York: Harper & Row,, 1968.

Pratkanis, Anthony, and Elliot Aronson. Age of Propaganda. New York: Henry Holt & Co., 2002.

Pribram, Karl H. Languages of the Brain. New York: Brandon House, Inc., 1971.

Quine, W. V., and J. S. Ullian. The Web of Belief. New York: Random House, 1970.

Ramachandran, V.s., and Sandra Blakeslee. Phantoms in the Brain. New York: Quill, 1999.

Rampton, Sheldon, and John Stauber. Weapons of Mass Deception. New York: Jeremy P Tarcher/Penguin, 2003.

Ramsland, Katherine. The Criminal Mind. Cincinnati, OH: Writer Digest Books, 2002.

Rank, Otto. Art and Artist. New York: W.W. Norton & Company, 1989.

Ravitch, Diane. The Language Police. New York: Vintage Books, 2004.

Rescher, Nicholas. Paradoxes. Chicago: Open Court, 2001. Rhees, Rush. Wittgenstein and the Possibility of Discourse. Oxford: Blackwell, 2006.

Rheingold, Joseph C. The Mother, Anxiety, and Death. Boston: Little, Brown and Company, 1967.

Riker, William H. The Art of Political Manipulation. New Haven: Yale UP, 1986.

Riso, Don R., and Russ Hudson. Personality Types. Boston: Houghton Mifflin Co., 1996.

Robertson, Robin, ed. Mortification. New York: Harper Collins, 2004.

Rogers, Peter. A Painter's Quest. Santa Fe, New Mexico: Bear & Company, 1988.

Rohmann, Chris. A World of Ideas. New York: Ballantine Books, 1999.

Rorty, Richard. Philosophy and the Mirror of Nature. Princeton, New Jersey: Princeton UP, 1980.

Rousseau, Jean-Jacques. The Social Contract. London: Penguin Books, 1968.

Ruitenbeek, Hendrik M., ed. Psychoanalysis and Existential Philosophy. New York: E.P. Dutton & Co., Inc., 1962.

Russell, Bertrand. Mysticism and Logic`. Totowa, Nj: Barnes & Noble Books, 1981.

Russell, Bertrand. The Analysis of Mind. Mineola, NY: Dover Publications, Inc., 2005.

Russell, Bertrand. The Problems of Philosophy. London: Oxford UP, 1974.

Sampson, Geoffery. The 'Language Instinct' Debate. London: Continuum, 2005.

Sanborn, Patricia F. Existentialism. New York: Pegasus, 1968.

Sanchez-Pardo, Esther. Cultures of the Death Drive. Durham and London: Duke UP, 2003.

Sardar, Siauddin, and Borin Van Loon. Introducing Cultural Studies. Lanham: Totem Books, 1998.

Sartre, Jean-Paul. Essays in Existentialism. Secaucus, New Jersey: The Citadel P, 1972.

Sartre, Jean-Paul. The Transcendence of the Ego. New York: The Noonday P, 1957.

Schapiro, Meyer. Theory and Philosophy of Art: Style, Artist, and Society. New York: George Braziller Inc., 1994.

Schmidt-Hellerau, Cordelia. Life Drive & Death, Libido & Lethe. Trans. Philip Slotkin. New York: Other P, 2001.

Schopenhauer, Arthur. Essay on the Freedom of the Will. Trans. Konstantin Kolenda. New York: Dover, 2005.

Schopenhauer, Arthur. The Will to Live. Ed. Richard Taylor. New York: Continuum Co., 1988.

Schopenhauer, Arthur. The World as Will and Idea. Vermont: Everyman, 2002.

Schopenhauer, Arthur. The World as Will and Representation. Trans. E.f. J. Payne. Vol. I. New York: Dover, 1969.

Schueler, G. F. Reasons & Purposes. Oxford: Clarendon P, 2003.

Schwartz, Jane. Grammar Power. 3rd ed. New York: Simon & Schuster, 2003.

Scott, Nathan A., ed. The Modern Vision of Death. Richmond, Virginia: John Knox P, 1963.

Scriven, Michael. Primary Philosophy. New York: McGraw-Hill Book Company, 1966.

Searle, John R. Minds, Brans and Science. Cambridge, Ma: Harvard UP, 2001.

Searle, John R. Mind. Oxford: Oxford UP, 2004.

Searle, John R. Rationality in Action. Cambridge, Ma: The MIT P, 2001.

Searle, John R. The Rediscovery of the Mind. Cambridge, Ma: The MIT P, 1992.

Shaw, Patrick. Logic and It's Limits. Oxford: Oxford UP, 2004.
Sheldrake, Rupert. The Presence of the Past. Rochester: Park Street P, 1995.

Shneidman, N. N. Dostoevsky and Suicide. Oakville, Ontario: Mosaic P, 1984.

Sluga, Hans, and David G. Stern, eds. The Cambridge Companion to Wittgenstein. New York: Cambridge UP, 1996.

Smelser, Neil J., ed. Karl Marx on Society and Social Change. Chicago: The University of Chicago P, 1984.

Smith, David W. Husserl. London: Routledge, 2006. Solomon, Andrew. The Noonday Demon. New York: Scribner, 2001.

Stafford-Clark, David. What Freud Really Said. New York: Shocken Books, 1997.

Stafford, Kenneth R. Basic Teachings of the Great Psychologists. Garden City: Dolphin Books, 1965.

Stern, David G. Wittgenstein on Mind and Language. New York: Oxford UP, 1995.

Storey, John. Inventing Popular Culture. Blackwell, 2003. Storr, Anthony, comp. The Essential Jung. Princeton: Princeton UP, 1983.

Strathern, Paul. Heidegger in 90 Minutes. Chicago: Ivan R. Dee, 2002.

Stroll, Avrum. Wittgenstein. Oxford: Oneworld, 2002. Tangney, June P., and Ronda L. Dearing. Shame and Guilt. New York: The Guilford P, 2002.

Tannen, Deborah. The Argument Culture. New York: Ballantine Books, 1999.

Tarnas, Richard. The Passion of the Western Mind. New York: Ballantine Books, 1993.

Taylor, Charles. Sources of the Self. Cambridge, Ma: Harvard UP, 2001.

Thevenaz, Pierre. What is Phenomenology? Ed. James M. Edie. Chicago: Quadrangle Books, 1962.

Todeschi, Kevin J. The Encyclopedia of Symbolism. New York: The Berkley Group, 1995.

Todorov, Tzvetan. Symbolism and Interpretation. Trans. Catherine Porter. Ithaca, Ny: Cornell Up, 1982.

Tolle, Eckhart. The Power of Now. Novato, Ca: New World Library.

Toulmin, Stephen. Return to Reason. Cambridge: Harvard UP, 2003.

Trask, R. L., and Bill Mayblin. Introducing Linguistics. Lanham, MD: Totem Books, 2002.

Trudgill, Peter. Sociolinguistics. 4th ed. London: Penguin Books, 2000.

Vallant, George E. The Wisdom of the Ego. Cambridge, Ma: Harvard UP, 1993.

Van Orman Quine, Willard. Word and Object. Cambridge: The MIT P, 1960.

Veblen, Thorstein. The Theory of the Leisure Class. New York: The Modern Library, 2001.

Voigt, Jurgen. Paradigms: Old and New. Santa Cruz, Ca: Aerial P, 1991.

Walker, Evan H. The Physics of Consciousness. Cambridge, Ma: Perseus, 2000.

Warburton, Nigel, ed. Philosophy Basic Readings. London: Routledge, 1999.

Weaver, Richard M. Ideas Have Consequences. Chicago: University of Chicago P, 1984.

Weber, Max. The Protestant Ethic and the "Spirit" of Capitalism and Other Writings. Ed. Peter Beahr and Gordon C. Wells. Trans. Peter Beahr and Gordon C. Wells. New York: Penguin Books, 2002.

Weber, Max. The Protestant Ethic and the Spirit of Capitalism. London: Routledge, 2002.

Weber, Max. The Sociology of Religion. Boston: Beacon P, 1993.

Wegner, Daniel M. Th Illusion of Conscious Will. London: Bradford Books, 2002.

Weitz, Morris, ed. 20th-Century Philosophy: the Analytic Tradition. New York: The Free P, 1966.

Wheelwright, Philip. Metaphor and Reality. Bloomington: Indiana UP, 1973.

Whitehead, Alfred N. Process and Reality. Ed. David R. Griffin and Donald W. Sherburne. New York: The Free P, 1985.

Whorf, Benjamin L. Language Thought and Reality. Ed. John B. Carroll. Cambridge: The MIT P.

Widdowson, H. G. Linguistics. Oxford: Oxford UP, 2003.

Williams, David L. The Mind in the Cave. New York: Thames & Hudson, 2002.

Williams, Meredith. Wittgenstein, Mind and Meaning. London and New York: Routledge, 2002.

Wilson, Colin. A Criminal History of Mankind. New York: Carroll & Graf, Inc., 1984.

Wippel, John F., and Allan B. Wolter, eds. Medieval Philosophy. New York: The Free P, 1969.

Wisdom, John. Paradox and Discovery. Berkeley: University of California P, 1970.

Wisdom, John. Philosophy and Psychoanalysis. Berkeley: University of California P, 1969.

Wittgenstein, Ludvig. Philosophical Investigations. Malden, Massachusetts: Blackwell, 2001.

Wittgenstein, Ludwig. Culture and Value. Chicago: The University of Chicago P, 1980.

Wittgenstein, Ludwig. Lectures & Conversations. Berkeley and Los Angeles: University of California P, 1972.

Wittgenstein, Ludwig. Lectures and Conversations on Aesthetics, Psychology, and Religious Belief. 2nd ed. Berkeley, 2007.

Wittgenstein, Ludwig. Ludwig Wittgenstein the Blue and Brown Books. New York: Harper Tourchbooks, 1965.

Wittgenstein, Ludwig. Remarks on the Philosophy of Psychology. Vol. II. Chicago: The University of Chicago P, 1980.

Wittgenstein, Ludwig. Tractatus Logico-Philosophicus. London: Routledge & Kegan Paul, 1961.

Wolff, Robert P. The Autonomy of Reason. New York: Harper Tourchbooks, 1973.

Young, Julian. Schopenhauer. London: Routledge, 2005.

Zgourides, George D., and Christie S. Zgourides. Sociology. Foster City: IDG Books Worldwide, Inc., 2000.

Zweig, Connie, and Jeremiah Abrams, eds. Meeting the Shadow. Los Angeles: Jeremy P. Tarcher, Inc., 1990.

Want to Learn More?

The assessments I do with people are more involved than simply identifying the Life Theme, but I've abbreviated them to keep things simple. If you'd like to learn more about assessment, please visit my website at www.JohnVoris.com.

www.ingramcontent.com/pod-product-compliance
Lightning Source LLC
Chambersburg PA
CBHW052033070526
44584CB00016B/2016